COMPUTER ARCHITECTURE: A MINIMALIST PERSPECTIVE

THE KLUWER INTERNATIONAL SERIES
IN ENGINEERING AND COMPUTER SCIENCE

COMPUTER ARCHITECTURE: A MINIMALIST PERSPECTIVE

William F. Gilreath

Phillip A. Laplante

Penn State University

Distributors for North, Central and South America:
Kluwer Academic Publishers
101 Philip Drive
Assinippi Park
Norwell, Massachusetts 02061 USA
Telephone (781) 871-6600
Fax (781) 871-6528
E-Mail <kluwer@wkap.com>

Distributors for all other countries:
Kluwer Academic Publishers Group
Post Office Box 322
3300 AH Dordrecht, THE NETHERLANDS
Telephone 31 78 6576 000
Fax 31 78 6576 474
E-Mail <orderdept@wkap.nl>

 Electronic Services <http://www.wkap.nl>

Library of Congress Cataloging-in-Publication

A C.I.P. Catalogue record for this book is available from the Library of Congress

Gilreath, W., Laplante, P./Computer Architecture: A Minimalist Perspective

ISBN: 1-4020-7416-6

Contents

Preface

This book examines computer architecture, computability theory, and the history of computers from the perspective of minimalist computing – a framework in which the instruction set consists of a single instruction. This approach is different than that taken in any other computer architecture text, and it is a bold step.

The audience for this book is researchers, computer hardware engineers, software engineers, and systems engineers who are looking for a fresh, unique perspective on computer architecture. Upper division undergraduate students and early graduate students studying computer architecture, computer organization, or embedded systems will also find this book useful. A typical course title might be "Special Topics in Computer Architecture."

The organization of the book is as follows. First, the reasons for studying such an "esoteric" subject are given. Then, the history and evolution of instruction sets is studied with an emphasis on how modern computing has features of one instruction computing. Also, previous computer systems are reviewed to show how their features relate to one instruction computers.

Next, the primary forms of one instruction set computing are examined. The theories of computation and of Turing machines are also reviewed to examine the theoretical nature of one instruction computers.

Other processor architectures and instruction sets are then mapped into single instructions to illustrate the features of both types of one instruction computers. In doing so, the features of the processor being mapped are highlighted.

In the final chapter, the applications for one instruction processors are studied, and similar phenomena in nature and future work are discussed.

For brevity, it is assumed that the reader is already familiar with digital logic, computer architecture, assembly language programming, and a high level language like C. In addition, some familiarity with discrete mathematics and the theory of computation would be helpful, although it is not necessary. In any case, many suitable reference sources, and a rather extensive glossary are provided at the end of the text.

Finally, a generic form of assembly language is used throughout the text so that familiarity with one processor or another is not necessary. This assembly language is similar to MOS Technologies 6502 microprocessor. Appendix A provides a summary of the generic instruction set.

Acknowledgments

The authors would like to acknowledge the following individuals who have inspired them through their scholarly thoughts, words and deeds. In particular they recognize Corrado Böhm, Alonzo Church, Henk Corporaal, Saul Dinman, John Hennessy, Giuseppe Jacopini, Doug Jones, Jack Lipovski, F. Mavaddat, S.W. Moore, G. Morgan, B. Parvani, David Patterson, Paul Rojas, Daniel Tabak, Alan Turing, W. L. van der Poel, and others for their work in one instruction computing and related areas.

The authors would also like to thank Nancy Laplante for copy-editing the manuscript and to the people at Kluwer Academic Press, especially Susan Lagerstrom-Fife, Deborah Dougherty, and Sharon Palleschi for their technical assistance.

Finally, Phil Laplante would like to thank his wife, Nancy, and children Christopher and Charlotte for tolerating his endless hours of detachment (both physical and mental) while working on this text and other projects.

Chapter 1

ONE INSTRUCTION SET COMPUTING
The Lure of Minimalism

Simplicity is the ultimate sophistication.

Leonardo da Vinci (1452-1519), Italian painter, draftsman, sculptor, architect, and engineer.

1.1   What is One Instruction Set Computing?

The single or one instruction set computer (OISC, pronounced, "whisk") is the penultimate reduced instruction set computer (RISC)[1]. In OISC, the instruction set consists of one instruction, and then by the orthogonality of the instruction along with composition, a complete set of operations is synthesized. This approach is completely opposed to a complex instruction set computer (CISC), which incorporates many complex instructions as microprograms within the processor.

A processor that is implemented with one instruction may appear to be lacking the necessary functionality to be seriously considered. Yet there are some interesting benefits in employing a one instruction computer. For example, hardware level functionality is simplified when implemented around a single instruction. This greatly simplifies the underlying implementation, as the same functional element is repeatedly used to form the processor core. Another advantage is that since all the instructions are the same, the instruction decoder circuitry and complexity can be eliminated.

---

[1] In the literature the acronym "OISC" is used rather to represent one instruction set computer or one instruction set computing rather than "SISC" for "single instruction set computer" or "SIC" for single instruction computer to avoid confusion with the more common meanings of those acronyms.

A one instruction computer architecture is also the most flexible, as instructions can be synthesized from the fundamental one, allowing for a customizable view of the processor instruction set. This allows for creating an instruction set that is well suited to a specific problem domain.

Finally, because a one instruction computer uses such simplified hardware it does not require a high degree of tailoring to a specific implementation. This leads to the possibility of hardware implementation using alternate materials to silicon.

1.2   Why Study OISC?

Even with the aforementioned benefits, it is unlikely that anyone would be motivated to build a working OISC. Indeed, OISC might be viewed as "just" a very specialized form of instruction set, one that is so rare that it is unlikely to be of interest. So, why study OISC? One possible answer is that although CISC and RISC are the preeminent instruction set schemes, OISC represents the "worse-case" and therefore is worthy of study as a curiosity.

There are also other reasons. For example, OISC is also very simple, so by examining its properties and features, greater insight can be found in the CISC and RISC architectures. In more complex and varied instruction sets, such features can be hidden.

OISC can also be used as a basis for comparing and contrasting existing instruction sets. Synthesizing the more complex instructions of a particular computer architecture or system is a way to evaluate the instruction set without reference to the architecture. Using OISC then, a more objective and independent metric for examining instruction sets is obtained.

Reconfigurable, or "programmable" complete architecture is a new technological trend. Part or all of the architecture can be reconfigured to organize the hardware resources more efficiently for the type of problem being solved. Here OISC allows for one instruction to work consistently with the underlying hardware, which changes for each problem. A more specific instruction set would limit how programmable a reconfigurable architecture could be, reducing the advantage of a reconfigurable computer.

Finally, OISC architectures provide an excellent paradigm for implementing traditional von Neumann computers using non-traditional materials. Simply put, by massive scaling of simple, single instruction elements, a practical computer can be built. This facet has important implications in nanocomputing, optical computing, biological computing, and in other types of computing involving "exotic" materials. This advantage is important since von Neumann architectures have a much larger body of software engineering results including programming languages, tools and methodologies than non-von Neumann architectures.

1.3   A Look Ahead

A book devoted to a specialized architecture like OISC needs to be compelling. Fortunately, the following important reasons for studying OISC have been introduced.

1. A one instruction set computer is simple and therefore readily suited to evaluation and experimentation.

2. A one instruction set computer is a special case so it highlights properties and features of instruction sets that might be masked in the richer instruction sets.

3. A one instruction set computer is a useful benchmark for comparing and contrasting existing instruction sets.

4. In reconfigurable or programmable architecture, one instruction set computers allows for remapping of functionality without changing the hardware.

5. A one instruction set computer provides an architectural framework for building traditional computers using non-traditional materials.

The remainder of this text is devoted to the discussion of these advantages.

1.4   Exercises

1. What is your reaction to the notion of a computer with only one instruction?

2. List three arguments against a computer with only one instruction.

3. Are there any other reasons for studying a computer with one instruction besides those previously mentioned?

Note: Save your answers to the following questions for future reference.

Chapter 2

INSTRUCTION SETS
An Overview

A good notation has a subtlety and suggestiveness which at times make it almost seem like a live teacher.

Bertrand Russell (1872-1970), British philosopher, logician, essayist, and social critic, best known for his work in mathematical logic and analytic philosophy.

2.1   Elements of an Instruction

An instruction set constitutes the language that describes a computer's functionality. It is also a function of the computer's organization[2]. While an instruction set reflects differing underlying processor design, all instruction sets have much in common in terms of specifying functionality.

Instructions in a processor are akin to functions in procedural programming language in that both take parameters and return a result. Most instructions make reference to either memory locations, pointers to a memory location, or a register[3]. The memory locations eventually referenced contain data, which are processed to produce new data. Hence, any computer processor can be viewed as a machine for taking data and transforming it, through instructions, into new information.

2.2   Operands

It is important to distinguish which operand is being referenced in describing an operation. As in arithmetic, different operations use different terms for the parameters to distinguish them. For example: addition has addend and augends, subtraction has subtractand and subtrahend,

---

[2] Traditionally the distinction between computer organization and computer architecture is that the latter involves using only those hardware details that are visible to the programmer, while the former involves implementation details at a lower level.

[3] An exception to this might be a HALT instruction. However, any other instruction, even those that are unary, will affect the program counter, accumulator, or a stack location.

multiplication has multiplicand and multiplier, and division has dividend and divisor.

In a generic sense, the two terms "operandam" and "operandum" can be used to deal with any unary or binary operation. The operandam is the first parameter, like an addend, multiplicand, or dividend. The operandum is the second parameter, like the augend, multiplier, or divisor. The following formal definitions will be helpful, as these terms will be used throughout the text.

Definitions

operandam – the first operand or parameter to an instruction.
operandum – the second operand or parameter to an instruction.
resultant   – the third parameter that is the result of the operation by the instruction.

2.3   Instruction Formats

The defining elements of instructions hint at the varying structures for organizing information contained within the instruction. In the conventional sense, instructions can be regarded as an n-tuple, where the n refers to the parameters of the instruction. Hence, an instruction is like a function in that it takes parameters and returns a result of the instruction. The n-tuples represent the number of parameters and how they are used.

Processor instructions must model algebraic or logical functions, of which there are both binary and unary kinds. Most of these functions however can be modeled as binary. For example, a unary minus of variable x can be thought of as a multiplication of the number by an implicit second parameter with the multiplicand as -1. Processor instructions can also follow this same approach of implicit parameters for an instruction, yielding the following format:

```
source, destination, result,next location
```

In the following sections, the instruction formats will be described beginning with the most general to the more specific. The format of an instruction provides some idea of the processor's architecture and design.

2.3.1   4-tuple Form

The most general instruction is a 4-tuple instruction. It is a binary instruction with a resultant, and the next location for the processor to go to after the instruction completes. A 4-tuple instruction is of the form:

```
op-code operandam, operandum, resultant, next instruction
```

Such an instruction could be termed a "GOTO" instruction type. It is the most flexible, allowing flow of control among any memory location addressable by the processor. It is very inefficient however because one-fourth of the parameters are not used by the current instruction.

The 4-tuple instruction is inefficient for another reason. Most machine instructions are sequential in nature, except for conditional branching, jump, trap, and interrupt service instructions. Therefore, for the majority of the time, the next memory address will hold the next instruction, making the information in this fourth field redundant.

2.3.2   3-tuple Form

A simplification of the 4-tuple instruction leads to the next form, the 3-tuple (or 3-address) instruction. The 3-tuple instruction is of the form:

```
op-code operandam, operandum, resultant
```

This is closer to a mathematical functional form, which would be:

```
resultant = op-code(operandam, operandum)
```

This form eliminates the fourth parameter, which instead can be handled by the program counter. Since all instructions have a next location, which is often sequential, it is far more efficient and convenient to compartmentalize this information into a dedicated part of the processor. In general, registers are used to serve such a purpose.

2.3.3   2-tuple Form

A 2-tuple form is a simplification (or complication depending on the point of view) of the 3-tuple form. The 2-tuple (or 2-address) form means that an architectural decision was made to have the resultant and operandum as the same. The 2-tuple instruction is of the form:

```
op-code operandam, operandum
```

or stated another way:

```
op-code source, destination
```

as a mathematical function the 2-tuple would be expressed as:

```
operandum = op-code(operandam, operandum)
```

Hence, the resultant is implicitly given as the operandum and stores the result of the instruction.

The 2-tuple form simplifies the information provided, and many high-level language program instructions often are self-referencing, such as the C language statement:

```
i = i + 1;
```

which is often abbreviated in the short, cryptic C form of:

```
i++;
```

This operation could be expressed with an ADD instruction in 2-tuple form as:

```
ADD 0x01, &i        /* 2-tuple */
```

where &i is the address of the i variable[4]. A 3-tuple instruction would redundantly state the address of the i variable twice, as the operandum, and as the resultant as follows.

```
ADD 0x01, &i, &i   /* 3-tuple */
```

However, not all processor instructions map neatly into 2-tuple form, so this form can be inefficient. The 80x86 family of processors including the Pentium® use this instruction format.

2.3.4   1-tuple and 0-tuple Forms

Some processors have instructions that use a single, implicit register called an accumulator as one of the operands. These so-called 1-tuple (1-address or accumulator) architectures are discussed in the next chapter.

Other processors have instruction sets organized around an internal stack in which the operands are found in the two uppermost stack locations (in the case of binary operations) or in the uppermost location (in the case of unary operations). These 0-tuple (or 0-address or stack) architectures can be found in programmable calculators that use postfix notation. Stack architectures are also discussed in the next chapter.

---

[4] This convention is used throughout the book.

2.3.5   Mixed Forms

Most processors use a mix of instruction forms, especially if there is an implicit register. The following, self-descriptive examples, illustrate this point.

```
CLI            /*  clear   interrupt  flag  in   status
               register in 80x86 */

INC $8000  /*  increment  memory  location  by  one  in
               68K */

ADC $8000  /*  add  accumulator  and  carry  to  memory
               location in 6502 */

NOP            /* no operation in 6502 or 68K */
```

2.4   Core Set of Instructions

In any processor architecture, there are many instructions, some oriented towards the architecture and others of a more general kind. In fact, all processors share a core set of common instructions. Ultimately, it will be shown that this commonality reflects the fact that all computer architectures vary in organization, but have equivalent power and functionality.

There are generally six kinds of instructions. These can be classified as:

- horizontal-bit operation,
- vertical-bit operation,
- control,
- data movement,
- mathematical/special processing,
- other (processor specific).

The following sections discuss these instruction types in some detail.

2.4.1   Horizontal-bit Operation

The horizontal-bit operation is a generalization of the fact that these instructions alter bits within a memory location horizontally. Bits within a memory word are altered in the horizontal direction, independent of one another. For example, the third bit in the operands would affect the third bit in the resultant. Usually, these instructions are the AND, IOR, XOR, NOT operations.

These operations are often called "logical" operators, but practically speaking, they are bit operations. Some processors have an instruction to specifically access and alter bits within a memory word.

2.4.2   Vertical-bit Operation

The vertical-bit operation alters a bit within a memory word in relation to the other bits. These are the rotate left, rotate right, shift right, and shift left operations. Often shifting has an implicit bit value on the left or right, and rotating pivots through a predefined bit, often in a status register of the processor.

2.4.3   Control

Both horizontal and vertical bit operations can alter a word within a memory location, but a processor has to alter its state to change flow of execution, and which instructions the processor executes[5]. This is the purpose of the control instructions, such as compare and jump on a condition. The compare instruction determines a condition, such as equality, inequality, magnitude, and so forth. The jump instruction alters the program counter (or in the 4-tuple the operandum is the conditional next instruction) based upon the condition of the status register.

Interrupt handling instructions, such as the 80x86's CLI, clears the interrupt flag in the status register, or the TRAP in the Motorola 68000 (also known by the shorthand designation 68K) handles exceptions. Interrupt handling instructions can be viewed as asynchronous control instructions.

2.4.4   Mathematical

The bit operation instructions can create the effects of binary arithmetic, but it is far more efficient to have the logic gates at the machine hardware level implement the mathematical operations. This is true especially in floating point and dedicated instructions for math operations. Often these operations are the ADD, SUB, MUL, DIV, as well as more exotic instructions. For example, in the Intel Pentium®, there are built-in graphics instructions for more efficient processing of graphics.

2.4.5   Data Movement

The I/O movement instructions are used to move data to and from registers, ports, and memory. Data must be loaded and stored often. For example in the C language, the assignment statement is:

---

[5] If this were not the case, the machine in question would be a calculator, not a computer!

```
i = c;
```

As a 2-tuple instruction it would be:

```
MOVE &c, &i
```

Most processors have separate instructions to move data into a register from memory (LOAD), and to move data from a register to memory (STORE). The Intel 80x86 has dedicated IN, OUT to move data in and out externally of the processor through ports, but it is a data movement instruction type.

2.4.6   Other Instructions

The only other kinds of instructions are those specific to a given architecture. For example, the 8086 processor has a LOCK instruction to indicate that the bus is locked. The 68000 has an ILLEGAL instruction, which does nothing but generate an exception. Such instructions as LOCK and ILLEGAL are highly processor architecture specific, and are rooted in the design requirements of the processor.

2.5   Addressing Modes

The addressing modes represent how the parameters or operands for an instruction are obtained. The addressing of data for a parameter is part of the decoding process for an instruction (along with decoding the instruction) before execution.

Although some architectures have ten or more possible addressing modes, there are really three basic types of addressing modes:

- immediate data ,
- direct memory location,
- indirect memory location .

Each addressing mode has an equivalent in a higher-level language.

2.5.1   Immediate Data

Immediate data is constant and it is found in the memory location succeeding the instruction. Since the processor does not have to calculate an address to the data for the instruction, the data is immediately available. This is the simplest form of operand access. The high-level language equivalent of the immediate mode is a literal constant within the program code.

2.5.2   Direct Memory Location

A direct memory location is a variable. That is, the data is stored at a location in memory, and it is accessed to obtain the data for the instruction parameter. This is much like a variable in a higher-level language- the data is referenced by a name, but the name itself is not the value.

2.5.3   Indirect Memory Location

An indirect memory location is like a direct memory location, except that the former does not store the data for the parameter, it references or "points" to the data. The memory location contains an address that then refers to a direct memory location. A pointer in the high level language is the equivalent in that it references where the actual data is stored in memory and not, literally, the data.

2.5.4   Other Addressing Modes

Most modern processors employ combinations of the three basic addressing modes to create additional addressing modes. For example, there is a computed offset mode that uses indirect memory locations. Another would be a pre-decrement of a memory location, subtracting one from the address where the data is stored. Different processors will expand upon these basic addressing modes, depending on how the processor is oriented to getting and storing the data.

One interesting outcome is that the resultant of an operational instruction cannot be immediate data; it must be a direct memory location, or indirect memory location. In 2-tuple instructions, the destination, or operandum-resultant must always be a direct or indirect memory location, just as an L-value in a higher-level language cannot be a literal or named constant.

2.6   Exercises

1. Are there other possible classifications for instructions in a given instruction set?

2. Try to construct a minimal set of addressing modes. Construct a set of the most elaborate addressing modes (or research an existing computer such as the VAX). What is the difference between the two?

3. Find a processor with unique, special instructions and, considering the typical application area for that processor, discuss the need for the special instruction.

4. What instructions must all processors share? What instructions would be unique to a processor's intended problem domain? Provide some examples.

Chapter 3

TYPES OF COMPUTER ARCHITECTURES
A Miminimalist View

Computers are useless. They can only give you answers.

Pablo Picasso (1881-1973), Spanish painter, sculptor, graphic artist, and ceramist.

3.1   Overview

It is inappropriate here to provide a complete review of basic computer architecture principles as the reader is assumed to have acquired these. Instead, as nomenclature can differ slightly, a few key components are reviewed for consistency of reference. In this regard, the glossary may also be helpful.

It is important to reiterate here that computer architecture provides a programmer's eye view of the computer. The instruction set addressing modes, number of registers, and so forth, are what interest the programmer. The internal organization of the hardware is the purview of the computer architect. However, in discussing one instruction set computers and how they might work, it is necessary to discuss some details of hardware implementation.

At the most abstract level, a basic computer consists of the following subsystems: a collection of input-output (I/O) devices, a main memory store, and a central processing unit (CPU) (Fig. 3-1).

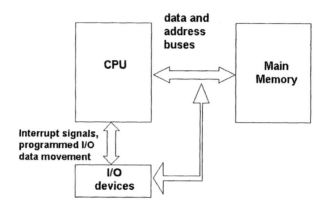

Figure 3-1. An abstract computer architecture.

Input and output occurs either through specific instructions for this purpose (programmed I/O) or through direct memory access (DMA). Interrupt signals are a form of input that causes the sequence of program execution to change and for code associated with the interrupt to be executed instead. I/O can also occur through virtualized memory locations via memory-mapped I/O, which is of particular interest in OISC architectures. Secondary memory storage devices are also treated as I/O devices.

It is beyond the intent of this text to discuss the various memory technologies and their performance characteristics. Instead, memory is viewed at the abstract level. It should be noted, however, that access time penalty for storing to or loading from memory is a significant contributor to instruction execution time cost. The function of the main memory store is discussed in the next chapter.

The CPU has many specialized registers and an internal micromemory, which are depicted without interconnections for simplicity in Fig. 3-2.

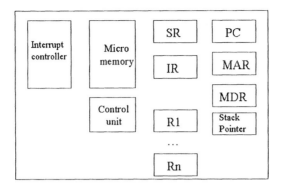

Figure 3-2. An idealized CPU showing some of the internal components without interconnections.

These internal components include the program counter (PC), which is a pointer into main memory, the instruction register (IR), which contains the opcode of the current instruction, and so on. For reference, Table 3-1 summarizes the components found in Fig. 3-2 along with their purpose.

Table 3-1. Certain components found in a typical CPU.

Component Name	Mnemonic	Function
control unit	CU	A complex circuit that orchestrates internal data movement and microinstruction sequencing.
general registers	Ri	The ith general register is addressable through operational codes, $i = 1, \ldots, n$.
instruction register	IR	Holds the opcode of the instruction that is currently being executed.
interrupt controller	PIC	A complex circuit that masks, latches, and prioritizes external interrupt signals.
memory address register	MAR	Holds the memory address to be read from or written to in the next memory bus cycle.
memory data register	MDR	Holds the data that was read from or is to be written to the memory address contained in the MAR in the next memory cycle.
micromemory	μ memory	A memory store that contains the microinstructions that form the complex logic of each macroinstruction.
program counter	PC	Points to the next instruction in main memory to be executed.
stack pointer	SP	Points to top of an internal or external stack structure.
status register	SR	Contains control information that is generated by prior execution of instructions.

3.2   A Simple Taxonomy

There are four general kinds of computer architectures in the widely used classification scheme given by Hennessy and Patterson [Hennessy98]. These are:

1. stack,
2. accumulator,
3. register-memory,
4. register-oriented (load-store).

3.2.1   Stack

In stack architectures the instruction takes the operands from an internal stack, not from memory or registers. The operands are moved from memory by pushing them onto the stack, and returned to memory by popping them off the stack.

The stack (or zero-address) architecture can be considered a 1-tuple instruction or 0-tuple, as 1-tuple instructions are needed for pushing from or popping to a memory address. The 0-tuple instructions are used for actual arithmetic and logical operations, which take the requisite operands from stack.

For example, the high-level C statement:

```
i++;
```

can be represented in stack architecture instructions as:

```
PUSH &i;
PUSH 0x01;
ADD;
POP  &i;
```

Note how data movement uses 1-tuple instructions, whereas the actual data processing instructions uses 0-tuple instructions.

Stack computer architectures allow for simplified compilers that generate machine code by building a simple parse tree and traversing it in post-order emitting PUSH {argument} code at the leaves and arithmetic opcodes at the root. This strategy eliminates the need for register allocation and allows for compact encoding of instructions.

Stack computer architectures are not used often in the pure stack concept, although all architectures support a run-time stack. The Java programming language, however, uses a stack architecture to implement the virtual machine and some commercial hand-held calculators are based on a stack architecture – those using reverse-polish-notation (RPN), for example.

3.3   Accumulator

Accumulator (or one-address) architectures are a register form, except that the primary register used is called the accumulator.

In early computers, hardware was relatively expensive, and therefore did not have as many registers as there are in modern computers. As all results would accumulate into this single register, it became termed an accumulator. Cambridge University's 1949 EDSAC (Electronic Delay Storage Automatic Calculator) was such a computer.

All operations and instructions use the accumulator, which then holds the resultant. The only other instructions are to load and store the accumulator with data.

For example, the high level C language statement:

```
i++;
```

Can be represented in accumulator architecture instructions:

```
LDA  &i;
ADDA 0x01;
STA  &i;
```

Some processor architectures have more than one accumulator, for example the MOS Technology 6502 microprocessor. This microprocessor used in the Apple II computer, had an accumulator and two "index" registers, which were actually accumulators. Part of the instruction set was designed to move data to and from the index and accumulator registers.

3.4   Register-Memory

The accumulator architecture suggests the possibility of employing additional registers that can be used by the instructions. Registers can hold operands in a very high-speed memory and can be accessed much more quickly than external memory. Providing high-speed general-purpose registers and special-purpose registers, therefore, becomes an advantage. This is the case in the register-memory (or 2-tuple address) architecture.

Some registers, such as status, program counter, are dedicated to a specific function, while others are data registers, or just general-purpose registers for use by processor instructions. Memory is still accessed to move data to and from registers, or as a part of the instruction, but the registers are like memory in that they are just accessed as part of the instruction operands.

To illustrate, the high level C statement of:

```
i++;
```

would compile to the following code in register-memory architecture instructions:

```
MOVE d0, &i;
INC  d0;
MOVE &i, d0;
```

Clearly then, moving frequently accessed memory to processor registers optimizes performance.

The IBM System/360® and DEC PDP-11® were among the first register-memory architecture based systems. The Intel 80386 and Motorola 68K processors are more recent register-memory processor architectures.

Register-memory is the most common architecture in use, with variations and specializations on the use of registers in a processor, winning out over pure accumulator or stack architectures.

3.5   Register-Oriented

Register-oriented computer architectures operate on the principle that all processor instructions reference registers as operands. Only data movement for loading and storing data is used. The register-oriented processor takes the optimization of keeping operands in the register to the extreme and makes it the primary means for computing. These architectures are also known as load-store, or 3-address.

Instructions reference only registers and the resultant (either another register or a memory location). The data is moved explicitly in and out of the registers for use.

For example, the high level language C statement:

```
i++;
```

In register-oriented architecture instructions it would be:

```
LOAD  r7, &i;
ADD   r7, 0x01, r7;
STORE r7, &i;
```

A primary focus of reduced instruction set computers, is to use such instructions that worked only within the register set. The PowerPC®, MIPS®, and SPARC® processors are examples of register-oriented processor architectures.

3.6   Exercises

1. List the advantages and disadvantages of the four computer architecture types in relation to each other. To answer this question it might be helpful to draw a matrix with the architecture types as both rows and columns, and fill in the cells.

2. The Java Virtual Machine (JVM) and Pascal p-machine use a stack architecture. Discuss the advantages of this approach.

3. The register-oriented architecture is sometimes referred to as a load-store machine. Explain the change in classification using load-store as opposed to general-purpose register.

4. Can the accumulator architecture be considered a specialization of the register-oriented machine architecture?

5. Give your own definition for computer architecture, and compare it to the definitions from other sources.

6. Is the Hennessy-Patterson taxonomy of computer architecture a software or hardware-oriented approach?

7. Formulate your own classification scheme for computer architecture. Describe your taxonomy and how the re-classification is similar and different from the standard classification scheme. Then take the standard classification and re-classify the different types.

8. A Harvard computer architecture uses a separate instruction bus, as opposed to the Princeton computer architecture, which does not. How does a Harvard computer architecture fit into Hennessy and Patterson's classification scheme?

9. Does the addition of a cache, bus, or virtual memory change the classification of a computer architecture? Why or why not?

Chapter 4

EVOLUTION OF INSTRUCTION SETS
Going Full Circle

It takes an endless amount of history to make even a little tradition.

Henry James (1843-1916), American-born writer of literature, psychology, and philosophy.

4.1 Motivation

To understand how OISC fits into the instruction set concept it is helpful to study the evolution of instruction sets. The emphasis on this synopsis is not comprehensive.[6] Instead, the focus is on key moments in computing history that impacted the nature of instruction sets.

4.1.1 "Big Iron" Computers

Early computers are often called "big iron" processors because of their use of vacuum tubes, electric relays, and bulk magnetic storage devices. They were also very large, often occupying an entire room. These devices appeared before the advent of microprocessors, VLSI integrated circuits, and in some cases solid-state electronics and the transistor.

Two of these early computers were the ENIAC in 1945, and Harvard/IBM Mark I, in 1944. These two machines were the first to attempt to automate computation, and were used as ballistics calculators during the Second World War.

4.1.1.1 ENIAC (1945)

The Electronic Numerical Integrator and Computer (ENIAC) computer was interesting in that it required re-wiring a plug board to program it.

---

[6] For example, two important early computers, the Atanasoff-Berry computer and Zuse's Z3 computer are omitted for brevity. Then again so are Pascal's calculating device, Jacquard's loom, Babbage's Difference Engine, and Hollerith's tabulating machine!

Hence, the hardware configuration impacted the software program. But, because it used vacuum tubes, it was an all-electronic and not an electro-mechanical computer as were some of its predecessors.

4.1.1.2   Harvard/IBM Mark I (1944)

The Harvard/IBM Mark I, developed by Howard Aiken, was also known as the Automatic Sequence Controlled Calculator. The Mark I, unlike the ENIAC, was an electro-mechanical computer; but the Mark I did not use plug boards for programming. The Mark I was used primarily for making ballistics tables, and had instructions dedicated to that purpose, such as the interpolate operation. The Mark I had minimum decision ability, this feature was later added with conditional subroutines in 1946.

Both early computers are memorable in that the underlying hardware often reflected the purpose of the machine. The machines were computational in nature, designed for high-speed calculation not general-purpose computing.

It is also an interesting historical footnote that the ENIAC was electronic but used a plug board, whereas the Mark I was electro-mechanical, but did not use plug boards.

4.1.2   First Stored Program Computers

John Von Neumann is credited with articulating the concept of a stored-program computer, that is, the separation of software from hardware [von Neumann45]. Most computers are based on this "von Neumann architecture."

In this view, programs can be data, and vice-versa. Treating instructions as data and vice-versa simplifies the hardware and software of computers. The two principles of the stored-program computer are:

1. Instructions are represented as numbers.

2. Programs can be stored in memory to be read or written just like numbers.

4.1.2.1   EDSAC (1949)

The EDSAC was the first of the "von Neumann" architecture computers, which implemented the stored program concept. The stored program concept was innovative, because it gave the conceptual framework for programmable devices that were general-purpose. The

EDSAC was the first computer to embody those concepts in the architecture.

4.1.2.2   IBM 704 (1954)

The IBM 704 was a model in the 701-series of computers built by IBM in the 1950s. This computer was important in that the architecture and instruction set influenced the development of the programming languages FORTRAN I, and LISP. Later computer architects included instructions in the instruction set to support high level language constructs.

The first high-level language, FORTRAN I, was developed by Backus and others at the time the 704 mainframe was in use[7]. FORTRAN was originally designed as a high-level language for the 704; at the time the idea was that different computers would have different high-level languages. There was a strong machine dependence, as the FORTRAN language designers included features from the 704 that were useful. FORTRAN I's control structures are based on the 704 instruction set.

Later, underlying computer architecture and instruction sets would reflect support for the concept of a "high-level computer language architecture," or support for higher-level languages at the processor level. McCarthy implemented LISP, like FORTRAN, on a 704. Two LISP functions, CAR and CDR follow from the 704-instruction set. The 704 had instructions for contents of address register (CAR), and contents decrement register (CDR). The naming convention followed into all dialects of LISP, including Scheme.

4.1.2.3   EDSAC2 (1958)

The EDSAC2 was not a direct successor to the first EDSAC. That is, it did not continue as a next generation model to the EDSAC. The computer architect, Maurice Wilkes, developed the idea of "microprogramming" which was implemented for the first time in the EDSAC2. To paraphrase Wilkes, "...the solution was to turn the control unit into a computer in miniature ...at the microlevel and by providing conditional micro-instructions" [Wilkes53]. When Wilkes invented microprogramming in the 1950s, fast memory was not yet available. Wilkes realized that the control processor could itself be viewed as a computer, albeit a much simpler one. The processor as a computer has very simple micro-operations that together can implement a macroinstruction that the programmer views as a

---

[7] Sheldon Best is credited by Backus with inventing the notion of registerization of frequently used variables. This optimization approach is the basis of RISC computing. In the 1980s Phil Laplante briefly worked with Best, who was still writing state-of-the-art compilers for avionics computers.

single instruction. Microcode is the internal code that causes the micro-operations to occur and implement a macroinstruction of the processor.

Microprogramming is akin to putting a computer inside a computer, so that more complex instructions can be implemented as a secondary program within the processor. The EDSAC2 employed this approach, using core-based read-only memory to implement the microcode.

4.1.3   Later Mainframes and Minicomputers

4.1.3.1   IBM System/360 (1964)

The System/360 mainframe was a landmark system in that it incorporated microprogramming. For the largest computer maker of the time, doing so legitimized the practice.

The System/360 also introduced the concept of "compatibility" of software, so if different models shared the same instruction set, then code for one platform could be run on the other platform. The concept of compatibility at the instruction set level would become ubiquitous in computer processor design. Henceforth, processors would provide new features but would also continue to support code for its predecessor.

4.1.3.2   IBM's 801 minicomputer (1975)

By the 1960s, John Cocke of IBM noted how infrequently processors utilized many of the complex operations they were constructed to perform. Cocke's insight was to hypothesize that it would be more efficient to rely upon only a few simple instructions. As Robert Cringley puts it, instead of a "walk-across-the-room-without-stepping-on-the-dog" instruction, rather there would be a set of simple instructions, "walk-walk-walk-step over-dog-walk-walk" [Cringley92].

IBM produced the first reduced instruction set computer in the late 1970s, with the 801-research project. John Cocke was the intellectual leader of a team of thirty computer scientists and engineers whose goal was to maximize the synergies of developing a new computer architecture with corresponding programming language, and operating system within the constraints of the cost of a minicomputer. The 801 used emitter-coupled logic, and was not unveiled until 1982. The 801 minicomputer was the progenitor of later IBM architectures, including the RS/6000, and PowerPC.

At the time of the 801 project there were similar ongoing projects at Stanford and UC Berkeley. These RISC computers are discussed more fully in Chapter 5.

4.1.3.3 DEC VAX 11/780 (1978)

The DEC VAX represented the pinnacle of complex instruction set evolution in the late 1970s. The architecture's instruction set directly supported operations and functionality of higher-level programming languages.

The VAX epitomized a concept that was popular at the time for high-level language computer architecture. The approach sought to eliminate the gap between high-level languages and computer hardware.

One failing of the VAX architecture was that it had too many instructions that supported features in high-level languages. But often the instructions did more than what was necessary. This semantic clash-giving too much semantic content to an instruction- made it possible to use the instruction only in limited contexts. More simply put, most complex instructions are too specialized for frequent use.

Hennessy and Patterson, for example, cite the VAX CALLS instruction, which performs many operations in the process [Hennessy96]. As Hennessy and Patterson note, "...attempts to support procedure call and activation stack management have failed ... they do not match the language needs or because they are too general and hence too expensive to use [Hennessy96]."

4.2   Evolution of Microprocessors

The following discussion concerning the development of microprocessors is not meant to establish the origination and invention of the microprocessor, which is a topic of considerable debate. Rather, the evolution of instruction sets on microprocessors that reflect the state at the time is emphasized.

4.2.1   Complex Instruction Set Microprocessors

4.2.1.1   Early 4-bit and 8-bit Microprocessors

Intel created the 4004, a 4-bit microprocessor, in 1970. This was later followed by the 8-bit 8008, and 8080 microprocessors. The instruction sets for the microprocessors followed the existing complex computer architectures of the time.

In 1976, the Z80 processor from Zilog was released. Its distinguishing feature was code compatibility with the 8080. New instructions were also added.

4.2.1.2   8:16 and 16-bit Microprocessor

There were other 8-bit microprocessors, including the 6502 from MOS Technology, the 6809 from Motorola. Intel released a "stop-gap" microprocessor, while developing the iAXP432 microprocessor. The processor was the 16-bit 8086, and the 8-bit external (16-bit internal) 8088. Both became the heart of the IBM PC, which went on to establish Intel's microprocessors as dominant.

4.2.1.3   32-bit Microprocessor

Later, 32-bit microprocessors were released, for example the i386 from Intel, which was upward code compatible with the previous 80x86 microprocessor. Motorola released the 68020, the successor to the 68000 (or 68K) microprocessor, which was a 16:32-bit architecture. Motorola's processors were used in the Macintosh and early Sun workstations.

4.2.2   Reduced Instruction Set Microprocessors

David Patterson pioneered reduced instruction set computers (RISC) at University of California at Berkley in 1981 where he developed the RISC I, and shortly thereafter, the RISC II computers. The design approach followed earlier work at Bell Laboratories on the CRISP C-Machine. John Hennessey of Stanford University, a Patterson collaborator, coined the term RISC.

John Hennessy designed and fabricated a RISC-like chip he called MIPS. Later he co-founded MIPS Computer Systems, an early RISC microprocessor manufacturer.

Sun developed the SPARC microprocessor as a replacement for the Motorola 68000 processors, which were used in its workstations. The SPARC followed the Berkeley RISC design approach. The SPARC was released in 1987, and its success convinced other companies of the legitimacy of the RISC approach.

4.2.3   Other Microprocessor Architectures

4.2.3.1   Very Long Instruction Word (VLIW) (1980s)

Very long instruction word (VLIW) is an instruction organization that breaks a processor instruction into a sequence of mutually exclusive primitive instructions. The primitive instructions can be executed in parallel when there are no resource dependencies amongst two or more instructions.

Microprocessors have "vertical" micro-operations for instructions in a sequence; VLIW has "horizontal" micro-operations for multiple functional units on the processor. VLIW aims to exploit instruction level parallelism, and gives the language compiler the task of ordering operations. The VLIW processor tends to be simpler because the control logic does not have to perform dynamic scheduling or reordering of operations. There is a simple one instruction launch per cycle. Software can do things that hardware could not do onboard the processor.

VLIW has limitations in that the compiler has to optimize and schedule the instructions to utilize instruction parallelism, and determine any resource dependencies or conflicts. Code must be aggressively optimized to produce enhanced performance, however there is the issue of compatibility with existing compilers available. Code size tends to be large, as the VLIW horizontal instructions pack multiple functionality of a RISC-like processor instruction into one very long machine word.

VLIW horizontal microcode existed in the early supercomputers such as the Control Data Corporation's CDC6600 and IBM System 360/91. The first true VLIW machines emerged in the early 1980s as mini-supercomputers from such companies as Multiflow, Culler, and Cydrome. Unfortunately these companies were not commercial successes, but the concept had been proven, and some of the first compiler technology had been implemented.

Later, the Intel i860 would be considered the first VLIW processor. The i860 depended upon the compiler rather than the hardware to sequence operations correctly.

Intel's Merced® or IA-64 processor instruction set is a derived form of VLIW. The IA-64 instruction set groups three instructions per bundle, and provides explicit dependency information.

Nowadays, the "politically correct" term for VLIW is explicitly parallel instruction (EPIC), the term VLIW having a bad connotation from the early failures with the technology. Also, VLIW technology is not only suitable for microprocessors. For example, Digital Signal Processor (DSP) chips have emerged that are based on the principles of VLIW processing.

4.2.3.2   Transmeta Crusoe (2000)

The Transmeta Crusoe processor is a recent development. Its primary feature is its "code morphing" capability, that is, the ability to translate microprocessor instructions on the fly, most notably the x86 instructions used in PC software.

The Transmeta Crusoe processor is a VLIW processor that executes four instructions per clock cycle, but uses software to perform the featured code morphing ability that has made it so versatile. The x86 instruction set is decoupled from the underlying hardware, so that changes to the hardware do not impact the legacy x86 software base. A new processor design only requires a change in the code morphing software to translate x86 instructions into a new native instruction set.

4.2.3.3   Reconfigurable Computing (1990s)

The advent of field programmable gate array (FPGA) technology, which allows for custom configuration at the digital gate level, has led to the development of re-configurable computing, or "programmable architectures." Reconfigurable computers emerged in the late 1980s and early 1990s, with research and funding from the government for problem-specific domains. The technology and the field are new. In fact reconfigurable computing is the first trend to a more "generalized" computer beyond the entrenched von Neumann architecture.

A reconfigurable architecture allows for the programmed interconnection and functionality of a conventional processor, with the added advantage that it can be tailored to the types of applications involved. Algorithms and functionality are moved from residing in the software side into the hardware side.

With one instruction set computing, processor architectures have come full-circle. The efficiency and efficacy of one instruction computing is that it uses the basic mechanism to carry out instructions: move data among the functional areas. This approach eliminates the need for microprogramming, while allowing the programmer or compiler to program the processor, much like the technicians did with the plug boards and cables of the ENIAC. The only difference is in the size of processors (VLSI can integrate millions of transistors), and the use of software rather than hardware.

It should be noted that reconfigurable computing follows the same idea as OISC, although it allows gate-programmability at the hardware level. Interconnecting in the hardware different types of functionality yields a programmable architecture. One instruction computing is the software approach to this same concept. The close association between OISC and the FPGA will be explored further in Chapter 11.

4.3   Timeline

The timeline shown in Fig. 4-1 depicts the processors and innovations discussed in this chapter.

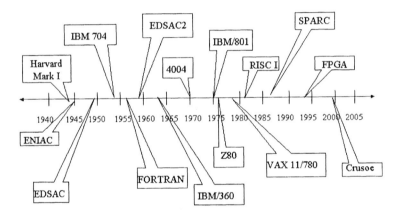

Figure 4-1. Milestones in the evolution of instruction sets.

4.4   Exercises

1. The early history of computers and the instruction sets focused on automating calculation. Do the instruction sets of the time period reflect that emphasis?

2. The stored-program concept led to general-purpose computers. What change in instruction sets followed the widespread adoption of the concept?

3. Compare and contrast instruction sets of the mainframes and minicomputers, with those of the microprocessor. Explain why there are similarities and differences in the instruction sets.

4. What are the significant new features found in the latest microprocessors and what has been the motivation for them? What instructions are shared with the previous generations' processors?

5. The types of computer architecture often influence the instruction sets. What have been the types of computer architecture over the years, and what architectures are the most prevalent now? What architectures seem to be poised to dominate in the future? What architectures have fallen into disuse?

6. Several high-level languages such as LISP, Forth, and Java have been directly implemented in hardware. Investigate a hardware-implemented language and examine the computer architecture. How does the instruction set follow the language?

7. Does the history of instruction sets reflect a design trend of the period, or an emphasis on high-level languages? Do the recent trends in instruction sets emphasize higher parallelism and instructions per clock?

Chapter 5

CISC, RISC, OISC
A Tale of Three Architectures

Know from whence you came. If you know whence you came, there are absolutely no limitations to where you can go.

James A. Baldwin (1924-1987), American writer and playwright noted for his novels on sexual and personal identity, and sharp essays on the civil-rights struggle in the United States.

5.1   CISC versus RISC

Complex instruction set computers (CISC) supply relatively sophisticated functions as part of the instruction set. This gives the programmer a variety of powerful instructions with which to build applications programs and even more powerful software tools, such as assemblers and compilers. In this way, CISC processors seek to reduce the programmer's coding responsibility, increase execution speeds, and minimize memory usage.

The CISC is based upon the following set of principles:

1. Complex instructions take many different cycles.
2. Any instruction can reference memory.
3. No instructions are pipelined.
4. A microprogram is executed for each native instruction.
5. Instructions are of variable format.
6. There are multiple instructions and addressing modes.
7. There is a single set of registers.
8. Complexity is in the micro program and hardware.

In addition, program memory savings are realized because implementing complex instructions in high-order language requires many words of main memory. Finally, functions written in microcode always execute faster than those coded in the high-order language.

In a reduced instruction set computer (RISC) each instruction takes only one machine cycle. Classically, RISCs employ little or no microcode. This means that the instruction decode procedure can be implemented as a fast combinational circuit, rather than a complicated microprogram scheme. In addition, reduced chip complexity allows for more on-chip storage (i.e., general-purpose registers). Effective use of register direct instructions can decrease unwanted memory fetch time

The RISC criteria are a complementary set of principles to CISC. These are:

1. Simple instructions taking one clock cycle.
2. LOAD/STORE architecture to reference memory.
3. Highly pipelined design.
4. Instructions executed directly by hardware.
5. Fixed format instructions.
6. Few instructions and addressing modes.
7. Large multiple register sets.
8. Complexity is handled by the compiler and software.

A RISC processor can be viewed simply as a machine with a small number of vertical microinstructions, in which programs are directly executed in the hardware. Without any microcode interpreter, the instruction operations can be completed in a single microinstruction.

RISC has fewer instructions, hence more complicated instructions are done by instruction synthesis. A sequence of instructions is composed to produce a complex instruction. When this is a frequently used instruction, the compiler's code generator can use a template of the instruction sequence of simpler instructions to emit code as if it were that complex instruction. Using different compositions of instructions, more complex instructions can be synthesized from a reduced instruction set base.

RISC needs more memory for the sequences of instructions that form a complex instruction. CISC uses more processor cycles to execute the microinstructions used to implement the complex macroinstruction within the processor instruction set.

5.2   Is OISC a CISC or RISC?

A OISC is like a CISC processor only in that at a higher-level of abstraction, the stream of instructions forms more complex instructions. Since there is only one instruction, the instruction itself needs not be part of the stored program. Instead, the organization of the operands, and how they are addressed in the memory space, decoded, and processed, represent the inherent complexity.

A OISC is much more like a RISC in the most obvious way, in fact, OISC has been called the "ultimate RISC" [Jones88]. RISC uses fewer, simple instructions in combination to create more complex functionality. OISC must use this approach to synthesize more complex instructions, as will be demonstrated.

Since OISC seems to have features of both CISC and RISC, it is still unclear if it is distinctly one or the other. Therefore, a more formal analysis is needed.

5.3   Processor Complexity

A measure of instruction set complexity is helpful in comparing the relative "power" of CISC, RISC, and OISC. To formalize this, take each instruction from the set of instructions, I, and form an association with each memory address, m, in the address space M, where $|M| = 2^n$, for some large positive n. The Cartesian product

$$C = I \times M \tag{5-1}$$

represents the set of all instructions and their possible locations in memory. This basic quantity will be used to generate a complexity measure for CISC, RISC, and OISC.

5.3.1   Complexity of CISC

Consider a CISC processor that supports 2-tuple, 1-tuple, and 0-tuple instructions. Typical instructions would be of the forms:

```
2-tuple instructions: ADD $1000, $2000
1-tuple instructions: INC $1001
0-tuple instructions: NOP
```

For the tuples greater than 0, it is necessary to create an instruction for each memory location used. Thus, a general-purpose ADD, SUB would become a very specific instruction for two memory locations. To elaborate, on an 8-bit processor, the ADD instruction would become:

```
ADD_0000:  ADD $00, $00
ADD_0001:  ADD $01, $00
```

And so forth until:

```
ADD_FFFF:  ADD $FF, $FF
```

This combination expansion is for one 2-tuple instruction. For all the n-tuples the Cartesian product with the memory space is needed to generate the entire set of instructions.

The mathematical formula for the complexity (cardinality of the set of all possible combinations) of this expanded instruction set, C, is:

$$C = i_2 \cdot 2^{2n} + i_1 \cdot 2^n + i_0 \tag{5-2}$$

where i_0, i_1, and i_2 are constants for the number of 0-, 1-, and, 2-tuple instructions respectively. n is the number of bits in the memory word. 2^n is the number of combinations of memory for a word size n. For a 2-tuple the complexity contribution is 2^{2n} because each instruction uses two parameters from the memory space of 2^n locations.

From a more general form of complexity is:

$$C = \sum_{t=0}^{k} i_t 2^{tn} \tag{5-3}$$

where k is the highest order tuple in the instruction set. While it is unlikely that $k > 4$, it is theoretically possible to have 5-tuple or higher instruction types where the resultant is placed in multiple destinations. In any case, for a 2-tuple architecture equation 5-3 is just equation 5-2.

5.3.2   RISC

Modeling the complexity of RISC is somewhat different. Here, the LOAD and STORE instructions theoretically hold exclusive access to the main memory space. The remaining instructions work only with the expanded general register set.

Using this reasoning, the complexity for a RISC architecture is:

$$C = 2 \cdot 2^n + i \cdot r = 2^{n+1} + i \cdot r \tag{5-4}$$

where i is the number of instructions including the LOAD and STORE, and r is the number of registers, which are characterized as a memory space.

5.3.3   OISC

A OISC has only one instruction, and it accesses the entire memory space. Hence $i = 2^0 = 1$. Thus the complexity of the OISC processor is:

$$C = 1 \cdot 2^n = 2^n \tag{5-5}$$

Note that out of the 2^n memory space, some of the memory locations are alias for registers of functionality. Hence, the memory space is less than 2^n, but because the registers act like memory locations, they are included in the overall complexity.

5.3.4   Comparing Complexity

The complexity measure for CISC compared to RISC has a much more rapid combinatorial expansion. RISC creates a sub-space of possible instructions and registers within the overall memory space. The load-store architecture embodied by RISC simplifies its overall complexity. Overall complexity for an infinite number of instructions is a power of 2, so comparison of complexity is in relative degrees of infinite combination.

A summary and comparison of the complexities is shown in Table 5-1.

Table 5-1. Summarizing instruction set complexity by combinatoric expansion, where 2^n is memory size, i_k represents the number of k-tuple instructions, and r is the size of the general register set.

Processor	RISC	OISC	CISC
Memory size		2^n	
$n=4$	$32 + i \cdot r$	16	$i_2 \cdot 256 + i_1 \cdot 16 + i_0$
$n=8$	$512 + i \cdot r$	256	$i_2 \cdot 65536 + i_1 \cdot 256 + i_0$
$n=16$	$2^{17} + i \cdot r$	65536	$i_2 \cdot 2^{32} + i_1 \cdot 65536 + i_0$
$n=32$	$2^{33} + i \cdot r$	131072	$i_2 \cdot 2^{64} + i_1 \cdot 2^{32} + i_0$

All three processors have exponentially sized instruction sets, and as the bit size of the processor grows, so does the complexity within the same complexity class. However, for fixed sizes of processors, such as 4-bit, 8-bit, 16-bit, 32-bit, and 64-bit, the generated complexities are constant. These constants relative to one another can provide insight into the complexity.

Consider for example graphing the complexities for three fictional computers one CISC, one RISC, and one OISC. Assume that the instruction set is such that for each type of instruction (0-tuple, 1-tuple, and so forth) there are ten instructions. Further assume that for the RISC processor that there are 64 general purpose registers available. Fig. 5-1 depicts a graph of the complexity function for memory size 2^n, $n=4, 8, 16$, and 32. The units could be bytes, kilobytes, megabytes, or gigabytes.

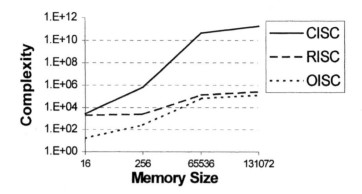

Figure 5-1. Measuring complexity for CISC, RISC, and OISC. Notice how the RISC processor behaves much like OISC as the memory space grows very large.

Viewed solely from the instruction combinational complexity, RISC looks very much like OISC. The fixed register set, fixed load-store instructions, and increased numbers of instructions add little to the level of complexity.

CISC represents the other logical extreme, complexity of instruction combination at its fullest. The size of the combination expansion of instructions and memory space quickly explodes upward. With a 32-bit word size processor, the CISC complexity borders on that of a 64-bit processor.

Hence, the complexity curves seem to imply that the OISC processor belongs in its own category. OISC shares properties from the RISC family of processors, and the CISC family. It can be viewed like either one, but it is clearly neither. OISC is the ultimate in simplification, with one instruction consistently and uniformly working in the memory space. The complexity is directly proportional to the memory space, which is in some ways, an ideal relation. This extreme approach creates a unique architecture that embodies both architectures.

5.4   Exercises

1. As RISC became ubiquitous experts predicted the "demise of CISC processors." However, CISC remains...why?

2. Both RISC and CISC are used to classify computer architectures based on the instruction set. Is it possible to classify the standard computer architecture types as RISC or CISC? Why or why not? (Hint: could there be a RISC stack architecture?)

3. What CISC processors have RISC like features, and vice-versa?

4. Is the RISC and CISC classification of computers still viable?

5. RISC seemed to follow the CISC computers as a change from the established approach. Could RISC have preceded CISC? Was there a reason why CISC was developed first?

6. Are some of the latest developments in computer architecture such as out-of-order execution, branch prediction, and integrated co-processors exclusive features of RISC or CISC?

7. CISC is often viewed as an approach to support high-level languages, whereas RISC tends to require better compilers for high-level languages. Is there a common design pattern to each perspective, or are they mutually exclusive?

8. One recent development is that of the explicitly parallel instruction computing, or EPIC architecture. (The Itanium® processor from Intel is the microprocessor product.) EPIC can execute more instructions in parallel to one another, therefore, in theory this would supplant RISC. Is this approach going to be "the death of RISC?" Does the parallel execution of instruction seem more CISC-like or RISC-like?

9. Another technical development is "hyper threading technology," which allows multiple execution of threads in parallel within a microprocessor. Is this a CISC-like feature from high-level virtual machine, or high-level language feature?

10. Computer processors are often influenced by higher-level abstractions (such as mutual exclusion). Is support for a higher-level features better or worse at the machine level?

11. Make a list of RISC features and CISC features. What is the intersection of the two sets?

12. What properties of one instruction computing are not found in the reduced or complex instruction sets?

Chapter 6

OISC ARCHITECTURES
Elegance Through Simplicity

The sciences do not try to explain, they hardly even try to interpret, they mainly make models. By a model is meant a mathematical construct which, with the addition of certain verbal interpretations, describes observed phenomena. The justification of such a mathematical construct is solely and precisely that it is expected to work.

John Von Neumann (1903-1957), Mathematician, physicst, and pioneer in fields such as game theory and modern computing.

6.1 Single Instruction Types

There are several theoretical models for OISC, of which subtract and branch if negative, MOVE, and the more primitive half adder architecture are the most important. The following sections describe these paradigms in some detail.

6.1.1 Subtract and Branch if Negative (SBN)

The subtract and branch if negative processor was originally proposed by van der Poel [van der Poel56a]. The instruction is of the format:

```
SBN operandam, operandum, next-address
```

where the operandum is subtracted from the operandam, and if the result is negative, execution proceeds to the next-address. Written as pseudo-code the SBN instruction takes the form:

```
operandam = operandam - operandum;

if(operandam < 0)
  goto next-address;
fi;
```

van der Poel indicated that both operands involved in the subtraction are given the result. Hence, the operandam and the operandum contain the difference of the subtrahend (operandam) with the minuend (operandum). The impact of the deviation from van der Poel's original model is unclear, except to simplify the complexity of the SBN operation.

Hennessy and Paterson give the alternative form [Hennessy98]:

```
sbn a,b,c   ; Mem[a]=Mem[a]-Mem[b]
            ; if (Mem[a] < 0) goto c
```

Moreover, the authors state that," ...no register and no instructions other than SBN," implying that the operands are not registers, but only memory locations [Hennessy98]. However, registers may be made available through memory mapping.

Subtract and branch if negative is akin to a 4-tuple instruction, with the next address being sequential from the instruction in the program counter. The third parameter of the instruction is the non-sequential next address if the result of the subtract is less than zero i.e., is negative. If the computer does not have a program counter, the fourth parameter could be the next address for continuation when the result of the subtractions is non-negative.

6.2   MOVE

A more "practical" kind of OISC offloads much of the processing to memory-mapped functional units. This MOVE instruction is of the format:

```
MOVE operandam, operandum
```

Written as pseudo-code, the move instruction takes the form:

```
operandum := operandam;
```

or more functionally:

```
copy(operandum, operandam);
```

Simply put, the contents of the operandam are moved to the operandum. The actual computation is achieved by the underlying hardware. In essence, the actual functionality is memory-mapped. The arithmetic unit is viewed as a contiguous block of virtual memory mapped to ADD, SUB, MULT, and other instructions. In addition, input and output is handled through memory-mapped I/O. Such an architecture is depicted in Fig. 6-1.

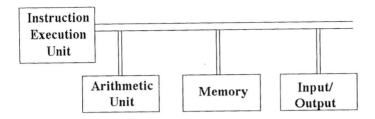

Figure 6-1. A MOVE OISC architecture depicting idealized arithmetic, instruction execution, memory, and I/O units. These are all implemented as memory-mapped locations.

The arithmetic unit consists of memory-mapped locations corresponding to the operands and resultant for the required arithmetic operations. For example, in Fig. 6-2 the arithmetic unit consists of addition, subtraction and twos complementation operations. Here memory locations FFF1 through FFEA (hexadecimal) are assigned to the operands and resultants.

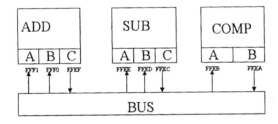

Figure 6-2. Arithmetic unit that can perform addition, subtraction or twos complementation. Note the memory location assignments for the operands and resultants.

MOVE is highly reminiscent of an accumulator-based architecture. Instead of a dedicated accumulator register upon which instructions take as an operand, the operandam is the accumulator contents, and the operandum is the instruction referencing the memory location where the actual hardware functionality is mapped.

6.2.1   Half Adder

A simple half adder digital logic circuit can be used to implement the SBN instruction and any arithmetic or data movement instruction [Laplante90]. Similarly, conditional branching can be implemented by presuming an implicit condition code, or status register [Laplante91b].

The idealized organization of such an architecture is shown in Fig. 6-3.

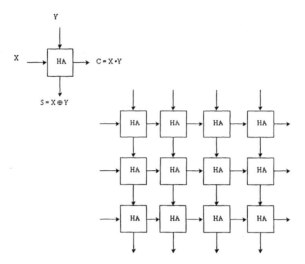

Figure 6-3. Configuration of a half adder OISC architecture showing basic half adder
element (upper left hand corner) and mesh connected elements.

Such a OISC implementation has several advantages. First, since only a
single type of logic element is employed the entire computer system can be
easily realized on a single, highly integrated chip or using FPGAs. In
addition, due to the homogeneous nature of the computer's logic elements,
the computer has possible implementations using alternative materials. This,
in turn, suggests possible paradigms for neural computing and artificial
intelligence.

Half adder architectures are more than simply a curiosity- they can be
used to implement real functionality, as will be shown later.

6.3   Comparing OISC Models

6.3.1   SBN

A subtract and branch if negative OISC is relatively complex instruction
made up of simpler operations. For example, viewing SBN as a sequence of
instructions:

```
SBN operandam, operandum, next-address

; resultant = operandum - operandam
SUB operandam, operandum, resultant
```

```
; compare result to constant zero
CMP resultant, 0x00

; branch if less than zero (negative)
BLT  next-address
```

SBN can be used to construct more complex instructions by instruction sequencing, and instruction parameterization. Instruction parameterization is choosing the parameters of the instruction so that the instruction behaves as another instruction. Two instructions that can be created by parameterization of SBN are:

```
;X = X - 0 no change, so nothing operation
NOP: SBN 0x00, X, Y

;X = X - X clears memory address X
CLR X: SBN X, X, Y
```

Instruction sequencing is choosing a sequence of instruction to create the behavior of another instruction. For example, to create two variations of the CLR instruction:

CLR X:
```
  SBN 0x00, X, Y;
  SBN X, X, Y;
  SBN 0x00, X, Y;
```

CLR Y:
```
  SBN 0x00, Y, Z;
  SBN 0x00, Y, Z;
  SBN    Y, Y, Z;
```

SBN can synthesize some instructions by instruction parameterization, but for the majority of more complex instructions, instruction sequencing is needed.

SBN is different from MOVE in that it is a 3-tuple form, but like a MOVE it only has operandam and operandum. The third parameter is the next-address if the difference in the operands is negative – it is not the resultant. Hence, like a MOVE instruction the operands implicitly are the resultants just as in a 2-tuple instruction.

6.3.2   MOVE

MOVE is a more "RISC-like" instruction. MOVE simply copies the contents of one memory location to another. The mnemonic "MOVE" is somewhat of a misnomer.

The MOVE instruction specializes by placing the required functionality at a specific memory address. MOVE does not compute or process data, it simply moves it to where it needs to go. This is more RISC-like in the sense that a RISC processor has an explicit load-store architecture, and all operations are performed on registers. In this case, the load-store is for an open memory space, and all operations are located at specific memory addresses within the address space.

MOVE can synthesize new instructions, but mostly by instruction parameterization. Instruction parameterization allows for operations to move data to the specific address of functionality. Once the basic instruction is created through parameterization, a sequence of instructions creates the behavior of the desired effective instruction.

The NOP and CLR instructions can be synthesized with MOVE:

```
; x := x copy back to itself
  NOP:  MOVE X, X

;move constant zero to location
  CLR X: MOVE 0x00, X
```

Both instructions are created through instruction parameterization. Likewise, using sequencing the CLR instruction can be created:

```
CLR X:
  MOVE 0x00, X
  MOVE X, X

CLR Y:
  MOVE Y, Y
  MOVE 0x00, Y
```

Both instruction parameterization and sequencing can be used to create the CLR instruction. The difference is that since only one memory location can be copied at a time, multiple instances of MOVE are necessary in the latter case.

6.3.3   Which OISC Instruction is Better?

MOVE is different from SBN in that it is a 2-tuple instruction. However, like SBN, the operandum is the resultant, or the destination of the move operation.

Table 6-1. Comparing Features of OISC Instructions.

	MOVE	SBN
orientation	data movement	data processing
instruction format	2-tuple	3-tuple
processor	RISC	CISC

Both OISC instructions SBN, and MOVE can implement the functionality needed for the one instruction of a OISC processor. The remaining question is, "Which OISC instruction is better?" The features of both SBN and MOVE are summarized in Table 6-1. SBN is more powerful as an instruction in that it synthesizes MOVE with only an implicit parameter, whereas MOVE requires many operations to synthesize SBN. MOVE is more easily synthesized with SBN, than vice-versa.

The comparison is better managed by defining "better" in terms of some criteria for OISC, not in terms of synthesizing one with the other.

Two possible criteria to evaluate OISC instruction are:

1. The instruction can synthesize all other instructions
2. There is consistency in use (processor and instruction synthesis)

Given these criteria, it should be clear that SBN is not "better" than MOVE. SBN cannot synthesize the bit-wise operations, and to do so requires an inconsistency in use. Hence, MOVE is "better than" SBN. Both are theoretically equally powerful, however, which will be shown later.

6.4   Variants of SBN and MOVE

There are variations of both SBN and MOVE, but in essence, the variations are minor changes to the basic model. SBN has variations upon the operations to subtract and branch, while MOVE has changes in word size operands.

6.4.1   Variations on SBN

6.4.1.1   van der Poel's Criterion

van der Poel's Criterion is a requirement that in the operation of SBN, both the operandam and operandum contain the difference computed between them. van der Poel put the restriction that both operands contain the result when the original instruction was proposed. A SBN operation that only stores the difference in the operandum is different from one that follows van der Poel's criterion. The difference will be illustrated later when the two models of OISC are used to implement one another.

6.4.1.2   Subtract

The subtract instruction is the most minimal form of the subtract and branch if negative instruction. Unlike the SBN instruction, subtract is a 2-tuple form instruction of the form:

subtract operandam, operandum

or in pseudo-code:

operandum := operandam – operandum;

In order to implement a branch, an index is subtracted from the program counter to generate the corrected effective branch address. A condition branch is performed by calculation of an offset into a lookup table, and then subtracting that value from the program counter.

The subtract instruction is simpler than the subtract and branch if negative, but what it simplifies it adds in complexity for branching and conditional branching.

6.4.1.3   Reverse Subtract and Skip on Borrow

The reverse subtract and skip on borrow (RSSB) is an unusual and interesting variation on the subtract and branch if negative instruction. It is a 1-tuple instruction, using an implicit accumulator register.

The reverse subtract and skip on borrow uses an accumulator, which is subtracted from the memory location, and the next instruction is skipped if there is a borrow in the status register. Some simple operations are not as simple when implemented with reverse subtract and skip on borrow.

The instruction has the form:

```
SBBN operand
```

or in pseudo-code:

```
accumulator := accumulator - operand
operand    := accumulator;

if(borrowFlag = true)
  program_count++2;
else
  program_count++;
fi;
```

6.4.2   Variations on MOVE

MOVE instruction variants are based mostly on the operand data size. A MOVE-based processor can move word, byte, double-byte, and so forth.

The variants change the complexity of using the MOVE instruction, but not its operation.

A full word MOVE is more flexible and efficient than a byte-oriented MOVE, which would require the ability to address bits within a location memory address. Then the byte-oriented MOVE can move bytes within a word of memory. The byte is more flexible, but is more complex, taking more instructions to accomplish what a single word-oriented MOVE instruction could perform.

6.5   OISC Continuum

The class of computers and processors that are in the category of one instruction set computers utilize a single instruction for all computation by the processor. The two most common instructions are the MOVE instruction, and the subtract and branch if negative instruction. These two instructions are not the only possible instruction for the one instruction computer. Other instructions are possible, such as NAND and branch on zero (NBZ).

The universe of OISC instructions can be illustrated graphically by the OISC continuum shown in Fig. 6-4.

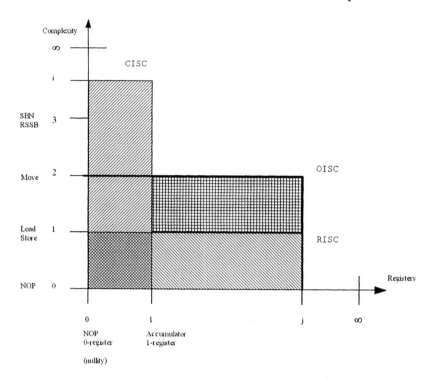

Figure 6-4. The OISC continuum.

Starting with the lower left hand side of the graph, is NOP instruction representing "nullity." NOP has zero complexity and uses no registers (not counting the PC). Moving to the right means increasing number of registers used in the instruction form. Moving upwards means increasing complexity in terms of the functionality of the instruction.

6.6   Exercises

1. Select a theoretical OISC model and explain its advantages and disadvantages. What types of applications or algorithms would be best suited to each theoretical model?

2. Is there a variant on one of the theoretical models that is better or worse than the original?

3. The majority of the theoretical models outside MOVE use an operation and a branch on a special case. Why? Is this the only way to implement a OISC, or are there other ways?

Chapter 7

HISTORICAL REVIEW OF OISC
Nothing New Under the Sun

History is indeed little more than the register of the crimes, follies, and misfortunes of mankind.

Edward Gibbon (1737-1794), English historian and scholar who authored "Decline and Fall of the Roman Empire."

7.1   Subtract and Branch if Negative (SBN)

7.1.1   van der Poel

A one instruction computer was first described by van der Poel in his doctoral thesis, "The Logical Principles of Some Computers" [van der Poel56] and in an article, "Zebra, a simple binary computer" [van der Poel59]. van der Poel's computer called "ZEBRA" for Zeer Eenvoudige Binaire Reken Automaat, was a subtract and branch if negative based machine. Standard Telephones and Cables Limited of South Wales in the United Kingdom later built the computer, which was delivered in 1958. For his pioneering efforts, van der Poel was awarded the 1984 Computer Pioneer Award by the IEEE Computer Society.

7.1.2   Mavaddat and Parham

The subtract and branch if negative instruction was later reused in an implementation of the very high definition language (VHDL), a high-level logic description language. Mavaddat and Parham called this computer "URISC: The Ultimate Reduced Instruction Set Computer" [Mavaddat88]. The processor was implemented entirely with VHDL. Armstrong and Gray later use the example in a VHDL textbook [Armstrong00].

7.1.3   Half Adder (1990)

Laplante used a hardware-oriented approach in implementing the subtract and branch if negative instruction by using hardware half-adders [Laplante90]. The intention was to provide a framework for alternate material computing.

Laplante also outlined some of the criteria for a complete instruction set, then showed how various operations could be derived from the half adder. For example, the XOR operation was used to derive addition, complement, preset, clear, and other operations. He later improved the conditional branching by presuming an implicit condition code or status register [Laplante91b]. From the register, it was shown how more elaborate functionality for branching could be implemented using the subtract and branch if negative operation.

7.2   MOVE-based

Elements of MOVE-based have been scattered in various computers from the early 1950s until recently, when an explicitly MOVE-based architecture was formulated.

7.2.1   English Electric DEUCE (1953)

The English Electric DEUCE (Digital Electronic Universal Computing Engine) of 1953 was a commercial version of Alan Turing's Pilot ACE (Automatic Computing Engine), which was developed in 1950. The DEUCE had two levels of storage, an acoustic mercury delay line main memory, and a magnetic drum for secondary storage. The binary form of the instruction set allowed the encoding of part of an instruction as a series of MOVEs, to and from the delay line memory and the magnetic drum.

7.2.2   GRI Computer GRI 909 Minicomputer (1969)

GRI Computer GRI 909 minicomputer developed a general-purpose minicomputer that incorporated a bus-based architecture. The architect of the computer was Saul Dinman, who published an article in 1970 describing it [Dinman70]. Dinman called the concept "The Direct Function Processor Concept." The path between the functional elements of the processor was programmable, so the movement of data between the different functional units was the central idea of how the processor operated. The instruction format included source, destination, and 4-bits to control the transfer of data through the system. Dinman received a patent on the "Direct Function Data Processor" in December 1971.

7.2.3   Burroughs B1700/B1800 Micro Architecture (1972)

These early microcoded machines included bit addressable memory, which allowed programming language implementations to choose the word length. This, in turn, enabled the computer to run a kind of virtual machine for each programming language supported. This close association of compiler and hardware technology in many ways anticipated the Java Virtual Machine.

7.2.4   New England Digital ABLE (1973)

New England Digital's ABLE was the creation of the company's co-founder Sydney Alonzo in 1973. The MOVE-based architecture was used to simplify the construction from basic transistor-transistor logic (TTL) integrated circuits. The instruction format had source and destination address locations encoded into a 16-bit word. The NED ABLE was used at Dartmouth in scientific laboratory systems, and later in AppleTalk routers.

7.2.5   Daniel Tabak/G. Jack Lipovski (1980)

Tabak and Lipovski mention a MOVE-based architecture, where the only instruction was a MOVE that worked in two-phases, used in digital controllers [Tabak80]. Tabak later wrote an important text on RISC processors [Tabak96].

7.2.6   Henk Corporaal/MOVE Transport-Triggered (1987)

Henk Corporaal of the University of Delft in the Netherlands led a research project to develop an advanced computer architecture around MOVE, extending it into the area of transport triggered architectures (TTAs). Ultimately the research culminated in a book on this architecture [Corporaal97].

7.2.7   Douglas Jones (1988)

Douglas Jones explored MOVE-based architectures and how they can fully realize a completely functional processor, one that is not sub-optimal [Jones88a], [Jones 88b]. Jones touches upon other previous architectures that contained MOVE functionality. Jones's work is later utilized in the programming of reconfigurable computer architectures that gained prominence in the late 1990s.

7.2.8   Reconfigurable Architectures

A OISC architecture can be remapped to organize the hardware resources more efficiently for the type of problem being solved. The recent emergence of field programmable gate arrays has impacted on the evolution of OISC. For example, Moore and Morgan built a OISC on a Xilinx field-programmable gate array that can be reconfigured to regenerate missing or faulty modules [Moore91]. Use of the FPGA in conjunction with OISC is discussed in Chapter 11.

7.3   Timeline

The timeline in Fig. 7-1 shows key moments in the history of one instruction set computing.

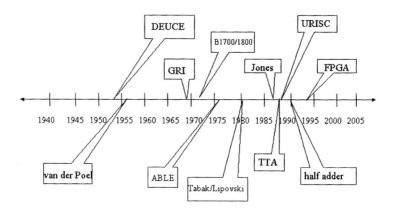

Figure 7-1. Milestones in the history of one instruction computing.

7.4   Exercises

1. Does the prior research in OISC emphasize one instruction, or is one instruction the conclusion from the research?

2. In what context does the SBN instruction arise? In what context did the MOVE instruction arise? Does any line of research suggest the suitability of one instruction over the other?

3. Does the current technology make one instruction more useful than it previously might have been? Why or why not?

4. For the prior work done with one instruction, is the author aiming for a hardware-oriented or software-based solution?

Chapter 8

INSTRUCTION SET COMPLETENESS
The Completeness Theorem

You cannot conceive the many without the one....The study of the unit is among those that lead the mind on and turn it to the vision of reality.

Plato (428-348 BC), Greek philosopher, one of the most creative and influential thinkers in Western philosophy.

8.1   Instruction Set Completeness

It is natural to assume that since a processor must perform many kinds of operations, having only one instruction is inadequate. This leads to the question of instruction set completeness, or "what is the minimal functionality of an instruction needed to perform all other kinds of operations in a processor?" This simple question touches upon the area of computation theory of effective computability.

Effective computability explores the principles of what determines if something is computationally tractable. The question of instruction set completeness, is to determine what is the minimal instruction set functionality necessary to have effective computability.

8.1.1   Turing Machine Model of Computation

A Turing machine is a mathematical model used to illustrate effective computability. In 1936 Alan Turing created a formal mathematical model to explore David Hilbert's "Decidability" or *Entscheidungsproblem* problem postulated in 1900 [Turing36]. Using the mathematical model, Turing was able to examine in greater detail tractable versus intractable calculation, and answer Hilbert's question that no general-purpose decidability algorithm exists. In doing so, Turing created a paradigm so powerful that it became the basis of computability theory. Alonzo Church, who arrived at the same conclusions as Turing simultaneously, extended the concept by showing that all models developed would be equivalent in power [Church36]. This informal assertion (often referred to as the "Church-Turing" thesis) is not subject to mathematical proof [Hennie77].

The Turing machine is a simple model consisting of an infinite tape and read/write unit that can write a single symbol at a time to the tape or read a symbol from the tape. While the symbols can be from any alphabet, a simple binary alphabet is sufficient. In any case, the read/write head moves one position either to the right or left depending on the symbol read on the tape at the position immediately below the read/write head. The read/write unit may also output a new symbol to the tape (overwriting what was previously there). Fig. 8-1 provides a simple illustration of the machine.

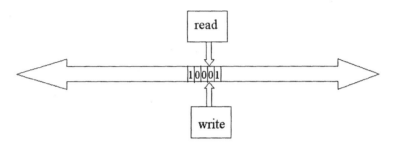

Figure 8-1. A simple, single tape Turing machine with binary encoding. The tape is infinitely long. The read/write head moves, and not the tape, to eliminate any concerns over the weight of an infinite-length tape.

There are many variations on the single tape, multiple character set Turing machine with infinite-length tape. There are machines that use various symbol sets and two or more tapes and even two-dimensional tapes. But all such machines can be shown to be equivalent [Turing36]. The most important observation is that anything computable by a Turing machine is computable by a more sophisticated and complex computer or processor.

8.1.2   Böhm-Jacopini Theorem

A Turing machine can be used as a fundamental model of computation, but it does not directly address the question of instruction set completeness. A Turing machine uses symbols, states, and infinite tape, which are analogous to memory addresses, and instructions in a processor, but not quite the same. The former two are used to examine the question of effectively computable; the other two are used to answer questions about minimal functionality expressed to be computable. The intention here is to examine completeness within the bounds of instruction sets. To help in this regard, there is another theorem more closely grounded to instruction sets that can assist – Böhm-Jacopini Theorem.

The Böhm-Jacopini theorem states that only the three grammar rules, sequence, selection, and repetition, are needed to construct any other instructions or a program [Böhm66]. Since by the Church-Turing thesis all processors are equivalent in power, the question of instruction set completeness is one of effectively constructing a program, or having the minimum functionality of instructions to do so.

The Böhm-Jacopini Theorem does for programming languages what Turing and Church did for models of computation – it proves that all programming languages are equivalent in power. The only distinction is the kinds of expressions of computation for different problem sets. Knowing this, it then follows speculatively that one instruction with a minimal set of functionality can be equivalent in power to as many instructions that together have the same minimal set of functionality.

8.1.3   Extended Böhm-Jacopini Theorem

There is another implicit grammar rule with the Böhm-Jacopini Theorem. This rule is that any new grammar rule can be added so long as it is based on some composition of the other three grammar rules. The fourth implicit rule can be termed "composition." Composition allows more complex grammars and more sophisticated programming languages to be constructed, like a meta-language. Hence different degrees of expressiveness can be had, but all are equivalent in expressive power.

The Böhm-Jacopini Theorem expresses the three fundamental principles as rules of a grammar. To simplify and provide a more narrow focus, the notion of rules of grammar will be dropped in favor of instructions in a hypothetical instruction set.

Each hypothetical instruction is denoted with:

```
address or label:    instruction ;comments
```

8.1.3.1   Sequence

In the hypothetical instruction set, sequence is expressed by a continuation or GOTO to the next address as:

```
x:     GOTO x+1
x+1:   GOTO x+2
...
x+k:   GOTO x+k+1
```

in a more general form sequence is denoted:

```
x:      GOTO x+1 ; goto next address
```

8.1.3.2   Selection

The selection or decision rule is expressed with a predication of continuation as a sequence (the next address) or out of sequence to another address. The continuation is a degeneration of selection into a sequence, and is the implicit action.

The explicit action is expressed as:

```
x:      GOTO on true x+k  ; otherwise goto x+1
...
x+k:    GOTO x+k+1  ; skips ahead over x+1 ... x+k-1
```

Selection also implies that a single bit, true or false status register is present. The instruction uses the condition of the status register to select forward, or to default to a sequence statement.

Finally, the degenerate behavior of sequence implies that there is a program counter for the next address that is updated by the instruction.

8.1.3.3   Repetition

Repetition is like selection in that it is a non-sequential continuation. Unlike selection, however, it is not predicated on a condition. Repetition is a non-sequential backward continuation. The repetition instruction is of the form:

```
x:      GOTO x+1          ; sequence
x+1:    GOTO x+2          ; sequence
...
x+k:    GOTO x+1 ;repetition from x+1 to x+k
```

One type of instruction that does not fit in with the Böhm-Jacopini Theorem's formation rules is of the form:

```
x:      GOTO x+1          ; sequence
x+1:    GOTO x+1          ; self-reference
...
x+k:    GOTO x+k+1        ;repetition from x+1 to x+k
```

That is, instead of advancing sequentially a sequence or repetition instruction references itself. It is not predicated on any condition, so the sequence continues. This self-reference is the common ground between sequence and repetition. If sequence were represented by the positive integers, and repetition by the negative integers, then sequence and repetition is of the form:

```
x:    GOTO x+m          ; sequence or repetition?
```

If $m < 0$, then the form is repetition; if $m > 0$ then the form is sequence.

An anomaly occurs, however, when $m = 0$. This is the case of unending self-reference in both sequence and repetition, which in effect, halts forward progress. Hence, the case where $m = 0$ is akin to a HALT instruction – something Böhm-Jacopini does not express in the formation rules.

8.1.4   Analysis of GOTO Instruction

Implementing the GOTO instruction set using the three formation rules of Böhm-Jacopini leads to some interesting observations.

1. The GOTO instruction modifies some register around where execution is occurring, which represents the state. This register is the program counter.

2. Selection degenerates into sequence, and sequence is PC = PC + m, where $m = 1$.

3. Repetition effects PC = PC + m, where $m < 0$

4. Selection effects PC = PC + m, where $m > 1$

5. A halt is a sequence PC = PC + m, where $m = 0$

6. Finally, selection is predicated on a status, so there is an implicit status register.

Expressed in a tabular form, the hypothetical GOTO instruction set is summarized in Table 8-1.

Table 8-1. A hypothetical GOTO instruction set.

Operation	Continuation	Conditional?	Operation	Continuation
sequence	x → x + 1	No	sequence	x → x + 1
selection	x → x + k; (k ≥ 1)	Yes	selection	x → x + k; (k ≥ 1)

Another way to express the table, is with the continuation equation in the form of:

x → x + k

and the continuation dependent on the value or range of k. The table is as shown in Table 8-2:

Table 8-2. State Machine Version of Hypothetical GOTO Instruction Set

Operation:	Continuation: x → x + k
sequence	k = 1
selection	k ≥ 1
repetition	k < 1
halt	k = 0

The hypothetical GOTO instruction set can be expressed by a Moore finite state machine with five states. The state transition function for this machine, with the alphabet, $\Sigma = \{0, 1\}$, is shown in Table 8-3.

Table 8-3. State transition diagram showing transitions (Moore state machine)

State	Next State	
	λ = 0	λ = 1
0	1	1
1	2	3
2	3	3
3	4	1
4	4	4

The graphical representation for this finite state machine is shown in Fig. 8-2.

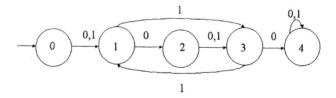

Figure 8-2. State transition diagram showing transitions (Moore state machine).

This state machine can be mapped to the hypothetical instruction set. The state represents the address of the instruction, and the next state function represents each instruction. If the next state function is constant regardless of the symbol, then the GOTO instruction is used. If the next state function is such that the next state is different based upon symbol, then a conditional GOTO is used.

Using this approach, the state machine maps into the hypothetical GOTO instruction set as:

```
0 GOTO 1            ; State 0, initial state
1 GOTO on true 3    ; State 1, default next address
                      is 2 for symbol 0
2 GOTO 3            ; State 2
3 GOTO on true 1    ; State 3, default next address
                      is 4 for symbol 0
4 GOTO 4            ; State 4, halts (the accepting state)
```

The state is represented in the hypothetical instruction by the program counter. The next state function is not the instruction, but a rule about whether the instruction causes selection or repetition. The conditional transition from one state to another in the finite state machine is controlled by the status register. The initial state is the starting address in the PC for the hypothetical instruction set. The HALT instruction is represented by a state that transitions back to the same state. Since every finite state machine must have a state and a next state function, so must the registers for a machine implementing the hypothetical GOTO instruction set.

The hypothetical GOTO instruction set can create any grammar formation or state transition for a finite state machine. Given an existing finite state machine, it can be mapped into the hypothetical GOTO instruction set, and in principle, vice-versa.

The hypothetical GOTO instruction set can be reduced to one instruction. But in doing so, the hypothetical GOTO instruction set is **not** complete. There are two instructions in the hypothetical GOTO instruction set:

```
; go to address x
GOTO x

; go to address x on true condition, else goto next
address
GOTO on true x
```

One of the hypothetical instructions, GOTO, is unconditional, the other GOTO on true, is conditional. Using the conditional instruction, the unconditional instruction can be derived. The important thing to note is that the status register determines if the GOTO on true instruction will GOTO address x. By setting the status register to true or false, the operation of the GOTO on true can be altered.

```
x:   GOTO on true  x+n      ; SR = true
x+1:GOTO on true   x+2      ; SR = false
...
x+n:GOTO on true x+1        ; SR = true
```

When the status register is true, the GOTO on true will go to the address specified. When false, it will go to the next address. If the address conditional upon the status register being true is the next address, it will go to the next address either way. Table 8-4 summarizes the behavior based upon the status register, and what the effective instruction is given.

Table 8-4. Hypothetical GOTO behavior based upon the status register and what the effective instruction is given.

Instruction	Status Register (SR)	Effective Instruction
x GOTO on true k	true	x GOTO k
x GOTO on true k	false	x GOTO x+1
x GOTO on true x+1	true	x GOTO x+1
x GOTO on true x+1	false	x GOTO x+1
x GOTO on true j	?	x GOTO j | GOTO x+1

The last row indicates that when the status register is not preset to true, or reset to false, then the GOTO on true instruction will behave like a selection formation rule. This is a subtle problem in the hypothetical GOTO instruction set, and the finite state machine- the code is pre-existing. The change of the status register to true or false will magically happen somehow, but not through any means of the instruction set. The next state function is independent of the hypothetical GOTO instruction set, so the instruction set is not complete. By contradiction to the single instruction, GOTO on true, demonstrates the incompleteness.

Here is the flaw in the hypothetical GOTO instruction set. The hypothetical GOTO instruction set can explicitly modify the PC (by the GOTO) and implicitly modify the PC (by the GOTO on true). So to change the state, the SR impacts the instruction GOTO on true, but cannot be modified explicitly or implicitly within the hypothetical GOTO instruction set. The previous analysis and the penultimate fact lead to some observations about instruction set completeness.

8.1.5   Principles of Instruction Set Completeness

There are five principles that govern instruction set completeness. Four focus on explicitly and implicitly modifying the state and next state functions. The fifth principle specifies that there is statefulness in the state and next state function. These principles, stated succinctly, are that in order for an instruction set to be complete it must satisfy the following properties:

1. The instruction set must be stateful by state and a next state function. (Statefulness Principle)

2. There must be an instruction to directly and explicitly modify state. (Explicit State Change Principle)

3. There must be an instruction to directly and explicitly modify next state function. (Explicit Next State Change Principle)

4. There must be an instruction to indirectly and implicitly modify state. (Implicit State Change Principle)

5. There must be an instruction to indirectly and implicitly modify next state function. (Implicit Next State Change Principle)

The principles seem self-evident, but are, in fact, subtle. State references the current address where the instruction set is executing, and can refer to the program counter, though this is not necessary. The next state function is for conditionals and selection, and can refer to the status register, but again this is not necessary. In fact, registers are just a convenient means to represent information in a processor architecture, and make that information available to the instruction set.

The principles do not state that one instruction every instruction can be complete. If one instruction is to form a complete set, however, it must satisfy the five principles.

The principles of instruction set completeness can be summarized in a statement, which in effect is a theorem about instruction set completeness.

Completeness Theorem

Any processor with a complete instruction set must be stateful of computation. That is, a means to alter the state or next state transition by explicit operation or by implicit computation is needed to deterministically affect processor state.

8.1.6   Applying the Principles

It was previously seen that the hypothetical GOTO instruction set was not complete. This fact, however, can be seen in another way. The hypothetical instruction set only satisfies some of the criteria for completeness.

The hypothetical GOTO instruction set satisfies the Statefulness Principle through registers for status, and a program counter. It also satisfies the Explicit and Implicit State Change Principles. That is, the GOTO x instruction directly alters the state by changing the next address in the program counter. The GOTO on true instruction indirectly modifies the program counter based upon the condition of the single-bit status register.

The hypothetical instruction set does not, however, satisfy the Explicit or Implicit Next State Change Principles, which would be represented by an instruction to change the single-bit status register. There are no instructions to preset to true, reset to false, or to setthe single-bit of the status register by a comparison. The GOTO instruction uses the next state function or status register, but there is no means within the hypothetical GOTO instruction set to alter it. Somehow, magically outside the instruction set the status register single-bit is either true or false. Failing to alter the next state function, that is the status register, illustrates something about the hypothetical GOTO instruction set: it does not perform any processing of information. In essence the GOTO x+1 at location x is a no operation or NOP instruction. The GOTO x+1 could be eliminated from the instruction set as a 4-tuple instruction with the next address or state as the fourth parameter. The GOTO if true would have the third and fourth parameters as the if-true GOTO address, and next address respectively.

The hypothetical GOTO instruction set can be re-written in 4-tuple form with a NOP instruction for the opcode, as shown in Table 8-5.

Table 8-5. The hypothetical GOTO instruction and 4-tuple equivalent.

Hypothetical GOTO Instruction	Equivalent 4-tuple Instruction
x GOTO x+1;	x NOP operandam, operandum, resultant, x+1;
x GOTO if true n;	x NOP operandum, operandum, n, x+1;

The hypothetical GOTO instruction set explicitly states flow of control while computing nothing. Hence, it might be called the ideal NOP instruction set. The mapping into the 4-tuple form illustrates that an explicit status register for a next state function, or program counter for a state function is not necessary.

8.1.7   Böhm-Jacopini Theorem Revisited

The Böhm-Jacopini grammar formation rules correspond with the principles of instruction set completeness. Sequence represents the linear transition to a successor state, or the increment of the program counter; so sequence directly alters the state. Repetition is the linear transition to a previous state by decrementing the program counter, which directly modifies the state. Selections can transition to a successor state, or degenerate into sequence and transition to a successor state in a linear fashion. Hence, selection modifies the state directly. The ability to select implies indirectly modifying the next state function so that for the given state the next state can change.

Interestingly enough, the Böhm-Jacopini Theorem does not imply any direct change to the next state function. However, next state change can be derived from selection. In order to do so, direct modification of the next state function is necessary to deterministically ensure that selection does degenerate into sequence. Hence, sequence from selection suggests that there is a direct means to modify the next state function.

Repetition is like the "inverse" of sequence. A single or multiple repetition transition can undo a series of sequence transitions among many states. It is then possible to have a selection that degenerates into repetition. Or generalizing further, selection could degenerate into repetition or sequence. It is possible to have one formation rule that encompasses the three explicit rules of the Böhm-Jacopini Theorem. By then degenerating deterministically, sequence and repetition can be constructed. In a sense then, only two formation rules apply, the encompassing rule, and the implied rule of synthesis by using multiple applications of the rule.

Table 8-6 summarizes the previous observations about the Böhm-Jacopini Theorem.

Table 8-6. A summary of properties of the Böhm-Jacopini Theorem depicted as a state machine.

State		Next State	
		$\lambda = 0$	$\lambda = 1$
sequence	x	x+1	x+1
selection	x	x+1	x+k
repetition	x	x+1	x−k
all-purpose	x	x+k	x−k

By choice of the input symbol lambda λ and the next state function parameter k, any of the three formation rules: sequence, selection, repetition can be formed.

Hence direct and indirect modification of the next state function (the status register) and the state (the program counter) allows any possible state under the simple alphabet $\Sigma = \{0,1\}$ to be reached from any other state. The program in question is determined by the exact nature of state transitions, the parameter k of the next state function, and the symbol λ.

8.2   A Practical Approach to Determining Completeness

The previous technique for showing the completeness or incompleteness of a given one instruction set illustrates some of the difficulties in applying the principles. It turns out that appealing directly to Turing's work is more helpful. This requires recognizing that if an instruction set can be shown to provide Turing Computability, then it proves all necessary functionality needed in both a theoretical and practical sense. This observation leads to the following definition.

Definition

An instruction set is complete if it is equivalent to a single tape Turing machine.

A Turing machine can be used as a fundamental model of computation; however, it is not really useful in determining practical completeness of a candidate OISC. The real question is, "how many computer instruction types are needed for a computer to be equivalent to a Turing machine?"

Recently, Rojas showed that four simple instructions (LOAD, STORE, INCrement, GOTO) are sufficient to evaluate any Turing computable function using self-modifying programs [Rojas96]. He also showed that conditional branching can be used to achieve unconditional branching, an important result for implementing "real " programs. This property is used to promote a workable definition of completeness.

PROPOSITION 1

A computer instruction set consisting of only the four 1-address instructions, LOAD, STORE, INCrement and GOTO is complete.

PROOF

Rojas provides an elegant proof, provided enough memory is available [Rojas96]. □

In fact, Proposition 1 is a well-known result.

PROPOSITION 2 (Böhm-Jacopini)

A complete computer instruction set capable of executing the three grammar rules: sequence, selection, repetition, can be used to construct any Turing computable program.

PROOF

See [Böhm66]. □

PROPOSITION 3

A complete instruction set can be used to construct any Turing computable program.

PROOF

To show this it must be shown that the sequence, selection, and repetition rules can be derived from LOAD, STORE, INC and GOTO. Fortunately, this is precisely the main result of the Böhm-Jacopini Theorem [Böhm66]. □

The net result of Propositions 1 through 3 is that any instruction set that can implement LOAD, STORE, INC and GOTO is functionally equivalent to a realization of a Turing machine. Hence, if a single instruction type can be found, and through clever manipulation can be used to induce the four instructions, such an architecture is not only theoretically complete, but functionally complete and powerful. This will be illustrated further throughout the text.

8.3   Completeness of Two OISCs

8.3.1   SBN

The SBN instruction as a set is complete and can be used to construct any Turing computable program.

To prove this it must be shown that SBN instruction can produce the 1-address instructions LOAD, STORE, INC and GOTO. Then by Proposition 2, it follows trivially that SBN is complete. By Proposition 3, it will then follow that any Turing computable program can be constructed.

Case 1: LOAD

Suppose it is necessary to load a memory location called R1 with the contents of memory location X, denoted (X). R2 is a scratch memory location (or register) and PC is a memory location containing the program counter, simply another memory location or register. Normally the program counter, auto increments and the next instruction is executed sequentially. In the cases where the result of an instruction is negative, placing the PC in the branch-address field insures that the next instruction in sequence is executed. The branch field can be changed to be other than the PC if a true branch is desired. In this way the LOAD is implemented as:

```
SBN  R2,R2,PC      ; clear R2
SBN  R2,X,PC       ; load -(X) into R2
SBN  R1,R1,PC      ; Clear R1
SBN  R1,R2,PC      ; transfer (X) into R1
```

Case 2: STORE

Suppose R1 contains the data to be stored at memory location X. R2 and Y play the same roles as in the case for LOAD. Then the STORE is implemented as:

```
SBN  X,X,PC        ; clear X
SBN  R2,R2,PC      ; clear Y
SBN  R2,R1,PC      ; put -(R1) into R2
SBN  X,R2,PC       ; store contents of R1 into location X
```

Case 3: INC

The INC instruction can be composed using an ADD instruction. Suppose it is desired to implement ADD R1,R2 that is, to add the contents of R1 and R2 and place the result in R1. Then with X as above yields

```
SBN  X,X,PC        ; clear X
SBN  X,R1,PC       ; put -(R1) in X
SBN  X,R2,PC       ; put -(R1)-(R2) into X
SBN  R1,R2,PC      ; clear R1
SBN  R1,X,PC       ; R1 contains (R1) + (R2)
```

The INC instruction is obtained by simply loading R2 with a memory location containing the value 1, using the LOAD instruction previously developed.

Case 4: GOTO:

Consider implementing GOTO X, where X is the target of the jump. This is easily implemented by forcing a negative result to a subtraction and placing X in the branch target field. Hence, if R1 contains 0 and R2 contains 1:

```
SBN R1,R2,X ; branch to X always
```

This has been shown that the SBN instruction set is compete and, hence, by Proposition 3 can be used to construct any Turing computable program.

8.3.2   MOVE

The MOVE instruction is complete and can be used to construct any Turing computable program.

To show this, consider a hypothetical MOVE processor with the operations shown in Table 8-7.

Table 8-7. A hypothetical MOVE processor.

Operation	Address
Addition	0x000000FF
Subtraction	0x000000FE
Comparison	0x000000FD
Logical Exclusive Or	0x000000FC
Logical AND	0x000000FB

And with the same hypothetical processor using the registers shown in Table 8-8.

Table 8-8. Registers for the hypothetical processor described in Table 8-7.

Register	Address
Program Counter	0x0000000
Processor Status	0x0000001
Accumulator	0x0000002

Other registers are possible, if specific information about the processor needs to be accessed at a memory address.

Most instructions are binary, taking two operands. In such a case, the MOVE instruction must move two operands, but the processor operation is located at only one memory address. This creates an operational inconsistency, unless two MOVE operations to the same memory location are required. By use of an accumulator register, a specialized area of memory can be created that is used by all binary operations on the OISC processor. Hence the accumulator register is added for operational simplicity and consistency.

In essence, with the hypothetical OISC processor based upon MOVE, an instruction takes the form of:

```
Operation operandam, operandum, resultant

  MOVE operandam, accumulator-address
  MOVE operandum, operation-address
  MOVE operation-address, resultant
```

Using this template the four necessary instructions, LOAD, STORE, INC and GOTO can be synthesized as follows:

Case 1: LOAD

By definition the MOVE instruction is a LOAD instruction if the operandam is a memory location and the operandum is a register.

Case 2: STORE

By definition the MOVE instruction is a LOAD instruction if the operandum is a memory location and the operandam is a register.

CASE 3: INC

The INC instruction can by synthesized from the ADD instruction easily. The ADD instruction is simply

```
ADD operandam, operandum, resultant:

  MOVE   operandam, 0x00000002
  MOVE   operandum, 0x0000FFFF
  MOVE 0x0000FFFF, resultant
```

Case 4: GOTO

The GOTO instruction is synthesized, as before, by adding the appropriate offset found in a table, to the program counter.

8.3.3   Half Adder

The half adder architecture is complete and can be used to construct any Turing computable program.

It is a simple exercise in digital design to show how a half adder can be used to form full-adders and ripple-carry adders. Half adders can easily be used to clear any register or memory location because of its implicit exclusive OR function. Further, it is a simple matter to "ADD" the contents of a memory location to an empty register to load it and ADD the contents of a register to an empty memory location to store. And it is was already shown how the ADD operation could implement INC and GOTO.

8.4   Exercises

1. Given an instruction set, under what conditions will instructions within the instruction set share an implicit instruction?

2. Take a simple algorithm (such as Fibonacci, Average, GCD, etc.) and express it with 2 of the 3 elements of a program defined by the Boehm-Jacopini Theorem. For example, implement GCD with only sequence and iteration.

3. Construct an instruction set that is incomplete, and explain why the instruction set is incomplete. As a variation, construct your own hypothetical machine, and explain why it is not a complete instruction model.

4. Describe the instruction set completeness theorem in more basic terms for the non-technical person.

Chapter 9

OISC MAPPINGS
Simulating Real Processors with OISC

Let him that would move the world first move himself.

Socrates (469-399 B.C.), Greek philosopher who was willing to call everything into question to find genuine knowledge.

9.1 Mapping OISC to Conventional Architectures

It has been noted that one of the advantages in studying OISC is that it can be used to benchmark existing instruction sets. In this chapter such a process is demonstrated for the four architecture types. The strategy involves mapping or simulating each architecture with a OISC architecture. This is done for both MOVE and SBN OISCs.

9.1.1 Stack (0-operand)

A stack-based architecture is not easily mapped to either basic type of OISC. Both MOVE and SBN use memory addresses, and SBN branches forward to another memory address. The memory address space is linear and accessible to each instruction.

A stack architecture, however, views memory as a stack, which is accessed not directly, but indirectly using PUSH and POP, which are inverse operations. PUSH writes to memory, and then moves to the successor location, and POP reads the memory location then moves to the predecessor location. Hence operands are implicit to the stack access, and not explicitly available.

Direct access to memory locations being used by the stack is not possible. Both the MOVE and SBN instructions require access to memory, and SBN the capability to continue execution ahead in memory. Nonetheless, partial mappings are possible.

9.1.1.1   MOVE

Because actual memory addresses are inaccessible directly, mapping a stack architecture is very difficult, if not impossible, using a MOVE OISC instruction. The duality of the PUSH and POP instructions means that each would have to have its own instruction, resulting in two instructions at a minimum.

Alternatively, a bit could be used to indicate read or write, but then for a MOVE it becomes:

```
MOVE push-flag x,y
MOVE 0 x, y      x:= y or push y, x;
MOVE 1 x, y      y:= x or pop  x, y;
```

Furthermore, a stack has an implicit count of operands, which would require an implicit stack counter register. The two instructions become a MOVE-PUSH or POP:

```
MPP 0, x;    MOVE Push or Pop, false so Push

MPP 1, x;    MOVE Push or Pop, true so Pop
```

In each case, MOVE has an associated bit, so there are really two MOVE instructions, not one.

9.1.1.2   Stack using SBN

SBN could be used to implement a stack architecture by using a bit to indicate SBN and PUSH if true, else POP.

```
; PUSH x-y, branch to z if (x-y) < 0
    SBN 0, x, y, z

; x = x - y
    PUSH x

; if x-y < 0
    GOTO z;

; POP  x-y, branch to z if (x-y) < 0,
; if x = x - y POP x
    SBN 1  x, y, z

; is it if x < 0? If so have to use y
; if x-y < 0 store   difference temporarily

    GOTO z;
```

The second case illustrates that SBN can push the difference of the two operands, but the difference is not pushed in the other variant; it is simply part of the decision to branch or continue to the next address. SBN with a POP means that the operandam does not contain the result of the difference operation. The operandum could follow van der Poel's criterion, that is, the operandam contains the top of the stack, and the operandum contains the difference.

Also, if van der Poel's criterion were not used in the SBN operation, then the difference would have to be stored in a temporary location, implying another implicit register. Whereas with a PUSH operation, the operandam contains the difference, and by van der Poel's criterion, so would the operandum. The POP operation, however, does not. Therefore, an SBN OISC stack architecture would need an implicit stack counter, and possibly a difference register.

Therefore, in the SBN OISC, like the MOVE OISC, two variants of the same instruction are needed. Clearly, OISC with stack architecture is impossible.

9.1.2   Accumulator

The accumulator architecture uses the accumulator as the central implicit register for all instruction operations that contain the operandam and result. The operandum is taken from memory or another register. The accumulator architecture is like the stack architecture in that it is not easily mapped to OISC. With an implicit register for all operations, the OISC instruction has to handle the accumulator as a special case, and not just a typical memory. The solution in implementing both types of OISC instructions is to rely less on the accumulator.

9.1.2.1   MOVE

With accumulator architecture, the accumulator is implicitly the register of choice with one of the operands and the result. A MOVE-based OISC the memory location of an operand contains the actual functionality. MOVE-based architecture with an accumulator is difficult because of the mixing of memory and accumulator. For the different kinds of MOVE, there is just an operand, or operandam with operandum.

MOVE-based accumulator architecture would have the instructions of the form:

```
MOVE y          ; Mem[y] = acc
MOVE x          ; acc = Mem[x]
MOVE x, y       ; Mem[y] = Mem[x]
```

There is the problem of disambiguating accumulator MOVEs from pure memory, and also whether the accumulator is the operandam or the operandum. Using Boolean bits, the distinction can be made so that the instruction becomes:

MOVE <only-memory-flag>,accumulator-operandam-flag x, y
```
MOVE  0  0  y
MOVE  0  1  x
MOVE  1  1  x,  y
```

With the addition of the 2-bit flags, the instruction does not consistently take the same number of operands. The addition of the 2-bits makes for four possible variants of the MOVE instruction, so in effect there are four instructions based on MOVE. Therefore, MOVE no longer provides a one instruction set computer.

One approach to avoid this problem is to map the accumulator to memory. A fixed, hard-wired memory address would access the accumulator register. Then the MOVE instruction can use pure memory operands for accesses. If the hard-wired address were in the operandam, or operandum would indicate if the access is moving data to or from the accumulator register.

If the specific address were 0x0000 then the MOVE is:

```
MOVE 0x0000, y    ; Mem[y] = acc
MOVE x, 0x0000    ; acc = Mem[x]
MOVE x, y         ; Mem[y] = Mem[x]
```

The actual processor could identify from the address if the accumulator is being accessed, and if so, as an operandam or operandum.

9.1.2.2   SBN

The SBN OISC architecture is trickier to map to the accumulator architecture. The SBN instruction takes the forms:

```
SBN y, z            ; accumulator is operandam

acc = acc - y
y = acc             ; by van der Poel's criterion
if( acc- y < 0)
     goto z;
```

```
SBN x,z                ;     accumulator is operandum


   x = x - acc
   acc = x             ; by van der Poel's criterion
   if( x - acc < 0)
        goto z;
```

There is a possible inconsistency in usage, depending upon if the accumulator is the operandam or the operandum, and if van der Poel's criterion is used in each case. To resolve this inconsistency, for each variant, the SBN, like the MOVE OISC, needs a flag to indicate if the accumulator is the operandam or the operandum. Then the new instruction would be of the form:

```
SBN <accumulator-operandam-flag operand>,goto-address


   SBN 1 y, z
   SBN 0 x, z
```

So for each variant, there is a single bit version, in effect creating two instructions based upon SBN.

There is also the problem of getting the value into the accumulator before the SBN uses the accumulator with a memory operand. Unlike the MOVE OISC, data must be transferred to (and possibly from) the accumulator. A certain amount of manipulation is needed to move data through the bottleneck of the accumulator, before the actual SBN instruction, to process the contents of the accumulator with another operand from memory.

A simple solution is to make the accumulator register not an implicit, but an explicit addressable memory location, similar to MOVE. Then SBN has the generality of accessing memory, along with using the accumulator. Using the MOVE OISC example, if the accumulator is 0x0000, then the instruction form becomes:

```
   SBN x, y, z

   SBN 0x0000, y, z     ; accumulator is operandam

   acc = acc - y
   y = acc             ; by van der Poel's criterion
   if( acc- y < 0)
        goto z;
```

```
SBN x, 0x0000, z          ; accumulator is operandum

x = x - acc
acc = x                   ; by van der Poel's criterion
if( x - acc < 0)
     goto z;
```

The processor can make the determination if the accumulator is the operandam or operandum, so a 1-bit flag is not needed.

9.1.3   Register-Register / Register-Oriented

The register-register (load-store) uses the registers as the default storage location of the operands for instructions. There is an explicit LOAD from memory and STORE to memory to access actual memory outside the processor. The register-register architecture is used by RISC systems to keep operands close to the processor, and simplify instruction use.

The register-register architecture is very similar to the accumulator-based architecture in that the latter is like a very narrow form of register-register with the only register being an accumulator. All instructions then work to the accumulator, having it as the implicit operand and resultant. The register-register architecture is one with many accumulators; so many that each has to be specified in the instruction. The loading and storing of operands is done by explicit instructions which access memory outside of the register set.

The conclusion is, therefore, that the accumulator based architecture is like register-register architecture in that it does not map easily to OISC.

9.1.3.1   MOVE

Mapping MOVE-based OISC to register-register architecture is difficult because memory is explicitly partitioned into registers and main memory. While implementing instructions to take only register operands leads to efficiency and performance, MOVE-based OISC only has the MOVE instruction, so requiring the instruction to take only operands from registers would be restrictive. Such a requirement would limit MOVE to working within the registers, and would require other instructions to MOVE data to and from the registers and primary memory.

One possible implementation is to require bits to distinguish the type of MOVE. The instruction would be of the form:

```
MOVE <mem-operandam flag> <mem-operandum> flag
     operandam, operandum

    MOVE 00, R0, R23        ; Reg[23] = Reg[0]
    MOVE 01, R13, $3000     ; Mem[3000] = Reg[13]
    MOVE 10 $8000, R1       ; Reg[1] = Mem[8000]
    MOVE 11 $3000, $8000    ; Mem[8000] = Mem[3000]
```

In essence, four different variants upon the essential MOVE instruction have to be created, corrupting the intent of having just one instruction.

One remedy to the mix and match of different kinds of memory is to normalize all of them as main memory. Registers are addressed as memory locations, so that the move only appears to be accessing a memory location.

Then the instruction would take the form:

```
MOVE operandam, operandum

    MOVE $0000, $0023       ; Reg[23] = Reg[0]
    MOVE $0013, $3000       ; Mem[3000] = Reg[13]
    MOVE $8000, $0001       ; Reg[1] = Mem[8000]
    MOVE $3000, $8000       ; Mem[8000] = Mem[3000]
```

9.1.3.2 SBN

Subtract and branch if negative OISC mapping to register-register architecture has the same difficulty as MOVE; the separation of memory into registers and primary memory requires distinguishing them in the operand fields, and the resultant field. The SBN instruction becomes:

```
SBN <operandam-flag><operandum-flag><next address-flag>
operandam, operandum, next-address
```

The parameters to the single instruction need to be identified as register or memory parameters. With three 1-bit combinations, there are eight possible variations on a single instruction; so one SBN instruction has proliferated into eight possible instructions.

SBN normally works on registers, and the results of the operation are returned to registers. The problem then arises, how to load and store the registers from main memory? Another technical problem is that SBN can continue to the next sequence in memory, but how does the sequence continue within the register set? In this case the next address can be in a register, but cannot continue in a register.

The problem, similar to the MOVE-based OISC, is that the inconsistent handling of the parameters to an instruction leads to variations upon the same instruction. The solution is, again, to access registers as memory locations.

One interesting conclusion is that by mapping registers to addressable memory locations, the explicit partitioning between registers and memory is lost. The load-store architecture is based upon explicitly loading and storing with registers from memory, so by making it transparent, no load-store is possible. In order to work with OISC of MOVE-based or SBN-based, the loading and storing of the register-register architecture must be abandoned.

9.1.4   Register-Memory

Register-memory is very similar to register-register, except that the boundary between registers and memory is not as explicit, nor do parameters have to be moved to and from registers and memory. The distinction is upon the type of memory, with a register being closer to the processor and therefore more efficient storage.

Again, both MOVE-based OISC, and SBN-based OISC have the same issue; the inconsistency of access to registers and memory. The solution is to take the registers and map them as a part of the memory space, making the accesses transparent to the instruction, but only apparent within the software.

9.1.5   Summary

OISC in SBN or MOVE-based form does not map completely to any type of computer architecture. It does map, however, with varying degrees of success. OISC requires a flat memory model, without a hierarchy of registers. It cannot distinguish access in reads or writes like the stack architecture, nor accesses to registers or a register in accumulator and register-register architectures. The architecture model for OISC, therefore, is a completely linear memory model, without registers or special access instructions.

9.2   Synthesizing Instructions

The next kind of mapping to be discussed involves the mapping of the one instruction onto others. This is the process of instruction synthesis. To be somewhat flexible, three addressing modes are considered, reflecting the more sophisticated addressing modes in other computer architectures.

The three addressing modes are (with the high-level construct in parenthesis):

1. direct memory (variable),
2. immediate data (constant),
3. indirect memory (pointer).

Instructions are synthesized partly by instruction parameterization, and then mostly by instruction sequencing. The combination of parameters and the modes of the parameters are used to create an effective instruction.

9.2.1   MOVE

Instructions are synthesized in a MOVE-based OISC by a sequence of instructions to create the desired functionality on the processor. This is the software level of instruction synthesis. At the hardware level on the processor, instructions are implemented in the underlying hardware and accessed by memory address.

MOVE has only the capability to copy, so moving to and from a memory address creates instructions, the address of the desired operation. Operations are accessed by memory address, and processor information to be moved to and from the system is passed through registers accessed by memory address.

Consider a hypothetical processor with the operations:

Operation	Address
Addition	0x000000FF
Subtraction	0x000000FE
Comparison	0x000000FD
Logical Exclusive Or	0x000000FC
Logical AND	0x000000FB

And with the same hypothetical processor using the registers:

Register	Address
Program counter	0x0000000
Processor Status	0x0000001
Accumulator	0x0000002

Other registers are possible, if specific information about the processor needs to be accessed at a memory address.

9.2.1.1   Binary Instructions

Most instructions are binary, taking two operands. In such a case, the MOVE instruction must move two operands, but the processor operation is located at only one memory address. This creates an operational inconsistency, unless two MOVE operations to the same memory location are required. By use of an accumulator register, a specialized area of memory can be created that is used by all binary operations. Hence the accumulator register is added for operational simplicity and consistency.

In essence, with the hypothetical OISC processor based upon MOVE, an instruction takes the form of:

```
Operation operandam, operandum, resultant

  MOVE operandam, accumulator-address
  MOVE operandum, operation-address
  MOVE operation-address, resultant
```

Using this template the following instructions can be synthesized using the table of memory addresses for operations and registers:

```
ADD operandam, operandum, resultant

  MOVE   operandam, 0x00000002
  MOVE   operandum, 0x0000FFFF
  MOVE 0x0000FFFF, resultant


XOR operandam, operandum, resultant

  MOVE   operandam, 0x00000002
  MOVE   operandum, 0x0000FFFC
  MOVE 0x0000FFFC, resultant


AND operandam, operandum, resultant

  MOVE   operandam, 0x00000002
  MOVE   operandum, 0x0000FFFB
  MOVE 0x0000FFFB, resultant


CMP operandam, operandum, resultant

  MOVE   operandam, 0x00000002
  MOVE   operandum, 0x0000FFFE
  MOVE 0x0000FFFE, resultant
```

The CMP or comparison operation suggests an important point. Normally a comparison operation will alter the bit flags in the processor status word. The comparison instruction synthesized does not have the implicit behavior. It can be done explicitly or implicitly as an implicit comparison instruction:

```
ICMP operandam, operandum, resultant

MOVE   operandam, 0x00000002
MOVE   operandum, 0x0000FFFE
MOVE   0x0000FFFE, resultant
MOVE   resultant, 0x00000001
```

The MOVE-based OISC processor exposes functionality to a level where software synthesis of instructions requires more control than a processor with built-in functionality.

9.2.1.2   Unary Instructions

The MOVE instruction template just discussed is for a binary operation. Unary operation can be synthesized from a binary operation with an implicit constant in the instruction. Hence explicit unary operations in hardware are redundant. For example, consider the following synthesized instructions:

```
NOT operand => XOR 0xFFFF…FFFF, operand, operand

CLR operand => AND 0x0000…0000, operand, operand

DEC operand => SUB 0x0000…0001, operand, operand
```

Subtract can be synthesized as:

```
SUBTRACT minuend, subtrahend, difference

NOT subtrahend
ADD minuend, subtrahend, difference
```

with NOT replaced with:

```
XOR 0xFFFF…FFFF, subtrahend, subtrahend
ADD minuend, subtrahend, difference
```

and so forth. Instruction synthesis by implicit operands is possible with a memory-oriented move-based OISC processor.

Creating these instructions from existing instructions synthesized from the MOVE-based instruction, yields:

```
NOT operand

   XOR 0xFFFF...FFFF, operandum, resultant

      MOVE    operandum, 0x00000002
      MOVE    0xFFFFFFFF, 0x0000FFFC
      MOVE    0x0000FFFC, operandum

   CLR operand

      AND 0x0000...0000, operand, operand
      MOVE    operandum, 0x00000002
      MOVE 0x00000000, 0x0000FFFB
      MOVE 0x0000FFFB, resultant

   DEC operand

      SUB 0x0000...0001, operand, operand
```

The decrement operation uses subtraction. Subtraction is the synthesis of the form:

```
      XOR 0xFFFF...FFFF, subtrahend, subtrahend
      ADD minuend,       subtrahend, difference
```

Expanding with the MOVE-based synthesized instructions:

```
   XOR
      MOVE    subtrahend, 0x00000002
      MOVE    0xFFFFFFFF, 0x0000FFFC
      MOVE    0x0000FFFC, subtrahend

   ADD
      MOVE    minuend,    0x00000002
      MOVE    subtrahend, 0x0000FFFF
      MOVE    0x0000FFFF, difference
```

In this example, subtraction is synthesized using implicit parameters, and by a sequence of MOVE operations to the provided functionality by the processor. An equally valid approach would be to provide the subtraction operation through the processor.

9.2.2   SBN

SBN implements addition by using the implicit subtraction capability, rather than moving to a memory location, which adds to operands. Like MOVE, the SBN-based OISC processor can use implicit parameters and a sequence of operations to synthesize new instructions.

Using the same register set as the hypothetical MOVE instruction:

Register	Address
Program counter	0x0000000
Processor Status	0x0000001
Accumulator	0x0000002

Then SBN can be used to synthesize the same instructions as with MOVE:

1. addition,
2. subtraction,
3. comparison,
4. logical exclusive OR, and
5. logical AND.

9.2.2.1   ADD

The ADD operation is synthesized by negating the operandum, then subtracting it from the operand, effectively adding the two operands. Algebraically this would be:

```
ADD(X,Y,Z)

Y := 0 - Y;
Z := X - Y  or Z := X - - Y which is
Z := X + Y;

ADD operandam, operandum, resultant

; negate the operandum, so operandum = -operandum
SBN 0x00000000, operandum, operandum, 0x00000000

; subtract operand from operandum, subtractin
; negative for addition
SBN operandam, operandum, resultant, 0x00000000
```

An ADD and accumulate instruction ADDA could be synthesized by making the resultant the accumulator, or:

```
ADDA operand, operandum

; negate the operandum, so operandum = -operandum
SBN 0x00000000, 0x00000002, 0x00000002, 0x00000000

; subtract operand from operandum, subtracting negative for
addition
; accumulator is resultant so accumulate

SBN operand,     0x00000002, 0x00000002, 0x00000000
```

9.2.2.2   SUB

Subtraction is the native operation of the SBN OISC, so subtraction is implemented easily:.

```
SBN operandam, operandum, resultant, 0x00000000
```

9.2.2.3   GOTO

The GOTO operand or next-address parameter can be the next address after the operation, so that negative or positive, the instruction flow proceeds sequentially.

9.2.2.4   CMP

The compare instruction works by comparing the two operands by subtracting. Before computing the difference, the resultant is subtracted from itself, clearing the register. Depending on the result of the operand subtraction, the constant value of greater-than, less-than-or-equal is moved into the resultant address. The result itself is meaningless; it is the jump to the particular point that is significant. This fact highlights the need for a "scratch" or null register/address where data is thrown away, much like the /dev/null in the Unix operating system. To illustrate the synthesis:

```
CMP operandam, operandum, resultant

  ; clear resultant
      SBN resultant, resultant, resultant
  ; determine if GT, or LE
      SBN operandam, operandum, temporary, ELSE
      SBN GT_CONSTANT, #0x0000000, resultant
  ; jump to after compare
      SBN #0x00000000, #0x0000001, FI
  ELSE: SBN LE_CONSTANT, #0x0000000, resultant
  FI: SBN #0x00000000, #0x0000000, temporary, 0x00000000
      NOP
```

An implicit comparison instruction can be synthesized by using the status register as the implicit resultant. The instruction sequence is then:

```
ICMP operandam, operandum

  ;clear resultant
        SBN 0x00000001, 0x00000001, 0x00000001
  ; determine if GT, or LE
        SBN operandam, operandum, temporary, ELSE
  ; copy constant to resultant
        SBN GT_CONSTANT, #0x0000000, 0x00000001
  ; jump to after compare
        SBN #0x00000000, #0x0000001, FI
  ELSE: SBN LE_CONSTANT, #0x0000000, 0x00000001
  FI:   SBN #0x00000000, #0x0000000, temporary,
0x00000000
  ; do nothing
        NOP
```

9.2.2.5 XOR

The XOR operation can be synthesized from the SBN, as the SBN uses an ADD operation, which is based upon XOR.

Taking the form of SBN:

```
NOT y
ADD x, y, z
```

Where NOT uses XOR with 0xFFFF...FFFF, and ADD is XOR. So then it becomes:

```
XOR #FFFF...FFFF, y
XOR x, y, z
```

9.2.2.6   AND

The logical AND operation is difficult and almost impossible to synthesize simply with SBN. The problem is that SBN is based upon XOR, and XOR is a closed operation. The XOR function is an inverse of itself, so hence it is a closed operation in regard to the set of bit-wise combinations and the resulting bits. This principle of exclusive-or closure makes it a non-trivial task to create the AND, OR logical operations with SBN.

However, all is not lost. The solution is to provide the AND, OR operations through the processor, much like MOVE. Then using the table of addresses for operations by MOVE:

```
AND operandam, operandum, resultant

    SBN operandam,  #0x00000000, #0x0000FFFB, 0x0000000
    SBN operandum,  #0x00000000, #0x00000002, 0x0000000
    SBN 0x0000FFFB, #0x00000000, resultant,  0x0000000
```

The instruction moves the operandam, and operandum to the accumulator and AND operation. Then the result is moved to the resultant. The MOVE functionality is implemented by subtracting zero.

9.2.2.7   Next-address Operand of SBN in Synthesizing Instructions

The synthesized SBN instructions indicate an interesting point of using SBN, the fourth parameter, the next-address parameter or GOTO operand. For instructions in which the branch is not to be taken, this can be redundant. One possibility is to use the next address (current address incremented by one) so that either way execution of the SBN instruction proceeds sequentially.

Making the next-address parameter (the GOTO operand) proceed sequentially can be difficult if implemented using SBN. Given any instruction, a prior instruction is needed to synthesize the GOTO parameter. This is modeled as:

```
ADD PC, +2, target-address, goto operand
    SBN operandam, operandum, resultant, target-address
```

The ADD instruction is the synthesis of two SBN operations, so it then is:

```
SBN 0x00000000, PC , operandum,  0x00000000
SBN operandam, operandum, target-address, 0x00000000
SBN operandam, operandum, resultant, target-address
```

Hence each SBN operation requires two previous SBN operations to create a continuation by the GOTO operand. This means that it can be very awkward and convoluted to create a predictable continuation.

Two alternatives to implementing GOTO operand continuation in the instruction set are:

1. an addressing mode with pre-increment, and
2. the compiler or assembler automatically completing the next-address field.

The pre-increment addressing mode simplifies things, by pushing the complexity of addressing operands to the processor. The SBN instruction is then:

```
SBN operandam, operandum, resultant, +(PC)
```

The alternative would be for the compiler or assembler to fill in the next-address operand with the address of the operation. In effect, a "macro" is preprocessed before generating machine code.

```
SBN operandum, operandum, resultant, CURRENT_ADDRESS +1;
```

One other alternative is when the next-address operand is not used as part of the instruction, to use the address of code that is specifically for debugging. Hence there is a "trap" capability when an instruction fails for some reason. Code created using SBN could have a debugging/trap address for operations in the debug version of the code, and a continuation to next address value for final release code.

The MOVE instruction can be modified to become a 3-tuple instruction with a next-address to add debugging capability. This would give some additional power to the MOVE instruction.

9.3   Code Fragments

To illustrate the instruction mappings further, several simple algorithms are coded using OISC instructions. These mappings represent, in essence, hand-compilation of a high-level language code into OISC assembly language. These mappings are undertaken for both SBN and MOVE OISCs.

9.3.1   High-Level Language C Structures

There are several high-level language constructs in programming languages that are used by software developers. The compiler and assembler generate the low-level machine code to implement the high-level construct. Examples of high-level language constructs taken from the C language are implemented to illustrate OISC code generation using MOVE and SBN.

9.3.1.1   If Statement

The C language construct is:

```
if(Boolean expression)
{
   then-statements (expression true)
}
else
{
   else-statements (expression false)
}
```

The else-construct is optional, and can be omitted. An example C language if statement:

```
if(x > y)
{
   y = x;
}
else
{
   x = y;
}
```

Any general assembly language would support symbolic variables, X and Y as memory addresses $1000 as $1001, respectively:

```
      CMP $1000, $1001
      BLE else
      MOVE $1000, $1001
      JMP endif
Else: MOVE $1001, $1000
endif:NOP
```

Implemented using MOVE-based OISC:

```
        MOVE &else, branch-target LE
        MOVE $1000, accumulator
        MOVE $1001, comparator
        MOVE comparator, status-word
        MOVE $1000, $1001
        MOVE &endif, PC
else:   MOVE $1001, $1000
endif:  MOVE accumulator, accumulator
```

Implemented using SBN-based OISC:

```
        SBN $1000,  $1001, temp, &else
        SBN $1000,  #00, $1001, nil
        SBN &endif, #00, PC, nil
else:   SBN $1001,  #00, $1000, nil
endif:  SBN PC,     #00, PC, nil
```

9.3.1.2 Loop Statement

There are three variants of a loop:

1. conditional pre-check (while),
2. conditional post-check (do-while), and
3. unconditional (infinite).

Since a while loop can be used to construct a for-loop (counted loop) the more general form will be used to illustrate OISC.

The simplest loop is the unconditional or infinite loop, which simply keeps iterating forever until it is exited, and program execution continues sequentially. In the C language it has the form:

```
while(1)
{
  while-statements;
}
```

The general machine code is:

```
while:NOP
      JMP &while
```

Implemented using MOVE-based OISC:

```
while:   MOVE $1000, $1000;
         MOVE &while, PC;
```

Implemented using SBN-based OISC:

```
while:   SBN $1000, 0, $1000, nil;
         SBN PC, &while, PC, &while;
```

The conditional pre-test loop is a while loop. The loop will be executed zero or greater times. The C while loop:

```
while(x > y)
{
   x--;
}
```

is implemented with general machine code as:

```
while:CMP $1000, $1001
         BLE &wend
         DEC $1000
         JMP &while
wend:    NOP
```

Implemented using MOVE-based OISC:

```
while:
         MOVE &wend, branch-target LE
         MOVE $1000, accumulator
         MOVE $1001, comparator
         MOVE comparator, status-word
         MOVE $1000, accumulator
         MOVE #0x01, difference
         MOVE accumulator, $1000
         MOVE &while, PC;
wend:    MOVE $1000, $1000;
```

Implemented using SBN-based OISC:

```
while:   SBN $1000,  $1001, temp, &wend
         SBN $1000, #0x01, $1000, nil; DEC $1000
         SBN PC, &while, PC, &while;
wend:    SBN $1000, 0, $1000, nil;
```

9.3.1.3 GOTO statement

The infamous GOTO statement allows for unconditional jump or branch within a high-level language program. The C language statement is:

```
x++;
goto label;
y++;
label:
x--;
```

In this example usage, the previous goto statement skips the statement y++.

The general machine code is:

```
        JMP &label;
        NOP;
label:  NOP
```

Implemented using MOVE-based OISC:

```
        MOVE &label, PC;
        MOVE $0000, $0000;
label:  MOVE $1000, $1000
```

Implemented using SBN-based OISC:

```
        SBN &label, 0, PC, nil;
        SBN $1000, 0, $1000, nil;
label:  SBN $0000, 0, $0000, nil;
```

9.3.1.4 Expressions

Expressions represent a series of operations upon data and variables that return a single value of the expression upon evaluation. Data and variables can be organized into sub-expressions, which are operated upon by expressions. There are two types of expressions:

arithmetic – return a numerical value, and
Boolean – return a Boolean (true or false) value.

9.3.1.4.1   Arithmetic Expressions

Consider the arithmetic expression:

```
j = x + 3 * (y - 1);
```

The expression part of the statement is: x + 3 * (y - 1), which expressed as general machine code is:

```
DEC $1000
MUL #0x03, $1000
ADD $1001, $1000
MOVE $1000, $1002
```

Where j, x, y correspond to memory addresses $1002, $1000, $1001 respectively.

Implemented using MOVE-based OISC:

```
MOVE $1000, accumulator;
MOVE #0x01, difference;
MOVE #0x03, product;
MOVE $1000, adder;
MOVE accumulator, $1003
```

Implemented using SBN-based OISC:

```
SBN $1000, 1, $1000, nil
SBN #0x03, 0, accumulator, nil
SBN $1000, 0, product, nil
SBN product, 0, $1000, nil
SBN #0x00, $1001, $1001, nil
SBN $1000, $1001, $1000, nil
SBN $1000, #0x00, $1003, nil
```

This is where the limit of SBN is illustrated. There is no easy means to implement multiply, so the MOVE-like functionality of an accumulator with functional addresses such as product is used. Subtracting and branching with a zero operandum creates an effective MOVE instruction.

9.3.1.4.2   Boolean Expressions

Consider the Boolean expression (x < y) && (y != 0). The C programming language uses an integer int value of 0 for false, non-zero for true. Other languages have an explicit Boolean type. In either form, the Boolean expression is still the same.

Expressed in general machine code, the Boolean expression is:

```
            CMP $1000, $1001
            BGE false;
            CMP #0x00, $1001
            BEQ false;
            MOVE #0x01, $1003
            JMP continue;
  false:    MOVE #0x00, $1003
  continue: NOP
```

Implemented using MOVE-based OISC:

```
            MOVE &false, comparator BGE-target
            MOVE $1000, accumulator
            MOVE $1001, comparator
            MOVE &false, comparator BEQ-target
            MOVE #0x00, accumulator
            MOVE $1001, comparator
            MOVE #0x01, $1003
            MOVE &continue, PC
  false:    MOVE #0x00, $1003
  continue: MOVE $1000, $1000
```

Implemented using SBN-based OISC:

```
            SBN $1000, $1001, temp, &false;
            SBN #0x00, $1001, temp, &true;
            SBN &false, #0x00, PC, PC;
  true:     SBN #0x01, #0x00, $1003, nil;
            SBN &continue, #0x00, PC, PC
  false:    SBN #0x00, #0x00, $1003, nil;
  continue: SBN $0000, #0x00, $0000, nil;
```

The Boolean expression has been modified to optimize it to the functionality of the SBN. To compare Boolean variable y that is memory location $1001 to zero, it is subtracted from it. If the result is negative, it is non-zero, so it branches to the location corresponding to true. Subtracting zero from $1001 would not have effectively branched no matter what the value of memory location $1001 or y.

9.3.2   Algorithms and Functions

9.3.2.1   Average

The average function takes an array of integers, and an integer size, and returns their average. The average function in C is:

```
#include <stdio.h>

int avg(int list[], int size)
{
    int x, sum;

    sum = 0;

    for(x=0;x < size;x++)
    {
        sum += list[x];
    }

    return (sum / size);
}
```

In generic assembly code:

```
_avg      NOP
          MOVE &list, $1000      ; avg(list[], size)
          MOVE size,  $1001
          MOVE #00,   $1002      ; sum = 0
          MOVE #00,   $1003      ; x = 0

_for      CMP $1001, $1003       ; x < size
          BGE _endfor
    ; {
          LDA $1000 ; acc = &list
    ; acc = acc + x or &list +x or list[x]
          ADA $1003
          STA $1004              ; temp = &list[x]
          LDA $(1004)            ; acc  = list[x]
          ADA $1002
    ; acc  = acc + sum or list[x] + sum
          STA $1002              ; sum  = acc
          INC $1003              ; x++
          JMP _for               ; }
_endfor   DIV $1001, $1002       ; sum = sum / size
          PUSH $1002             ; sum on return stack
          RET                    ; return from routine
```

The average function in MOVE-based architecture:

```
_avg    MOVE $0, $0                    ; nop
        MOVE &list, $1000              ; avg(list[], size)
        MOVE size,  $1001

        MOVE #00,   $1002              ; sum = 0
        MOVE #00,   $1003              ; x = 0

_for    MOVE &_endfor, ge_target       ; branch >= _endfor
        MOVE $1001, accumulator        ;  x < size
        MOVE $1003, comparator

        MOVE $1000, accumulator        ; acc = &list
        ;acc = acc + x or &list+x or list[x]
        MOVE $1003, adder
        MOVE accumulator, $1004        ; temp = &list[x]

        MOVE $(1004), accumulator      ; acc  = list[x]
        ; acc = acc + sum or list[x] + sum
        MOVE $1002, adder
        MOVE accumulator, $1002        ; sum  = acc
        MOVE #01, accumulator          ; x++
        MOVE $1003, adder
        MOVE accumulator, adder

        MOVE &_for, program_counter; }

_endfor MOVE $1001, accumulator        ; sum = sum / size
        MOVE $1002, divider
        MOVE accumulator, $1002
        MOVE $1002, $(param_stack_ptr); sum on return stack
        MOVE #01, accumulator
        MOVE $param_stack_ptr, adder
        MOVE accumulator, $param_stack_ptr
        MOVE $run_stack_ptr, $temp     ; return
        MOVE #1, accumulator
        MOVE $run_stack_ptr, subtractor
        MOVE accumulator, $run_stack_ptr
        MOVE $temp, program_counter
```

9.3.2.2   Binary Search

The binary search function takes an array of sorted integers, a size, and a key, and then returns the index into the array where the key is found. If not found, a sentinel value is returned.

The function works by iteratively computing the mid-point of the array, and comparing the key to the value at that index. From the comparison, the mid-point is recomputed to move half-way up or down the array, until either the key matches the value, or the midpoint equals the lower and upper indices of the array.

The binary search algorithm in C is:

```c
#include <stdio.h>

int bsearch(int list[], int size, int key)
{
    int low = 0;
    int high = size - 1;
    int mid;
    int flag = list[0] - 1;
    int last = -1;
    mid = ( low + high ) / 2;

    while(mid != last)
    {
        last = mid;

        if( list[mid] > key )
        {
            mid = (mid + low) / 2;
        }
        else if( list[ mid ] < key )
        {
            mid = (mid + high) /2;
        }
        else
            return mid;
    }
    return flag;
}
```

In generic assembly code:

```
_bsearch  NOP
    MOVE &list,  $1000    ; binarysearch(list[],
    MOVE size,   $1001    ; size,
    MOVE key,    $1002    ; key)
    MOVE #0,     $1003    ; low = 0
    MOVE $1001, $1004     ; high = size
    DEC $1004             ; high-- or high = size - 1
    MOVE $(1000), $1005   ; flag = list[0]
    DEC $1005             ; flag-- or flag = list[0]-1
    MOVE #-1, $1005       ; last = -1
    MOVE $1004, $1007     ; mid = high
    DIV #02, $1007        ; mid = high / 2

_while  CMP $1007, $1006; while(mid != last)
    BNE _do
    JMP _wend


_do
    MOVE $1007, $1006       ; last = mid
                           ; compute list[mid]
    LDA $1000              ; acc = &list
    ADA $1007              ; acc = list[mid]
    STA $1008              ; temp = &list[mid]
    LDA $(1008)            ; acc = list[mid]
    CMA $1002             ; if list[mid]
    BGT _keygt            ; > key
    BLT _keylt            ; < key
    MOVE $1007, $1008     ; temp = mid
    JMP _end

_keygt
    ADD $1003, $1007       ; mid = mid + low
    DIV #02, $1007         ; mid = mid / 2
    JMP _while

keylt
    ADD $1004, $1007       ; mid = mid + high
    DIV #02, $1007         ; mid = mid /2
    JMP _while

_wend   MOVE $1005, $1008 ; temp = flag

_end    PUSH $1008         ; return temp (flag or mid)
        RET
```

The binary search algorithm in MOVE-based architecture:

```
_bsearch MOVE $0, $0              ; NOP
      MOVE &list, $1000           ; binarysearch(list[],
      MOVE size,  $1001           ; size,
      MOVE key,   $1002           ; key)

      MOVE #0,    $1003           ; low = 0
      MOVE $1001, $1004           ; high = size

      MOVE #01, accumulator       ; high-- or high = size - 1
      MOVE $1004, subtractor
      MOVE accumulator, $1004
      MOVE $(1000), $1005         ; flag = list[0]
      MOVE #01, accumulator       ; flag-- or flag = list[0]-1
      MOVE $1005, subtractor
      MOVE accumulator, $1005
      MOVE #-1, $1005             ; last = -1
      MOVE $1004, $1007           ; mid = high
      MOVE #02, accumulator       ; mid = mid / 2
      MOVE $1007, divider
      MOVE accumulator, $1007

_while
      MOVE &_do, ne-target        ; while(mid != last)
      MOVE $1007, accumulator
      MOVE $1006, comparator
      MOVE &_wend, program_counter

_do
      MOVE $1007, $1006           ; last = mid
                                  ; compute list[mid]
      MOVE $1000, accumulator     ; acc = &list
      MOVE $1007, adder           ; acc = list[mid]
      MOVE accumulator, $1008     ; temp = &list[mid]
      MOVE $(1008), accumulator   ; acc = list[mid]
      MOVE &_keygt, gt_target     ; > key
      MOVE &_keylt, lt_target     ; < key
      MOVE $1002, comparator      ; if list[mid]
      MOVE $1007, $1008           ; temp = mid
      MOVE &_end, program_counter
```

```
_keygt
   MOVE $1003, accumulator       ; mid = mid + low
   MOVE $1007, adder
   MOVE accumulator, $1007
   MOVE #02, accumulator         ; mid = mid / 2
   MOVE $1007, divider
   MOVE accumulator, $1007
   MOVE &_while, program_counter

_keylt
   MOVE $1004, accumulator       ; mid = mid + high
   MOVE $1007, adder
   MOVE accumulator, $1007
   MOVE #02, accumulator         ; mid = mid / 2
   MOVE $1007, divider
   MOVE accumulator, $1007
   MOVE &_while, program_counter
_wend
   MOVE $1005, $1008                          ; temp = flag
_end
    MOVE $1008, $(param_stack_ptr)    ; PUSH return

temp (flag or mid)
   MOVE #1, accumulator
   MOVE $param_stack_ptr,  adder
   MOVE accumulator, $param_stack_ptr
   MOVE $run_stack_ptr, $temp        ; RET
   MOVE #1, accumulator
   MOVE $run_stack_ptr, subtractor
   MOVE accumulator, $run_stack_ptr
   MOVE $temp, program_counter
```

9.3.2.3   Fibonacci Sequence

The Fibonacci series is an infinite progression of natural numbers generated by the function, f with $f_0 = 1$, $f_1 = 1$ and $f_n = f_{n-2} + f_{n-1}$ for all other positive integers.

The Fibonacci function computes the nth Fibonacci number for all numbers in the series. The Fibonacci series is recursive in nature, but here is implemented iteratively. The function computes the desired Fibonacci number by iteratively computing forward in the series, until the desired number is reached, which is then returned.

The Fibonacci number function in C is:

```c
#include <stdio.h>

int fibonacci(int index)
{
        int fib_first;
        int fib_next;
        int fib_temp;
        int i;

        if(1 == index || 2 == index)
        {
            return 1;
        }

        fib_first = 1;
        fib_next  = 1;


        for(i=2;i < index; i++)
        {
            fib_temp  = fib_next;
            fib_next  = fib_first + fib_next;
            fib_first = fib_temp;
        }

        return fib_next;
}
```

In generic assembly code:

```
fib    NOP
   ; (int index) parameter pass by value
       MOVE index, $2000
       CMP #01  , $2000          ;  index == 1
       BEQ _basecase
       CMP #02  , $2000          ;  index == 2
       BEQ _basecase
       JMP _startfib

basecase
       MOVE #01,   $2002         ;  return 1 or fib_next=1
       JMP _endfor

startfib
       MOVE #1,    $2001         ; fibfirst = 1
       MOVE #1,    $2002         ; fibnext  = 1

       MOVE #2,    $2004         ; i = 2
startfor
       CMP $2004, $2000          ; i < index
       BGE _endfor               ;
                                 ; {
       MOVE $2002, $2003         ;fib_temp = fib_next
   ;fib_next=fib_next+fib_first
       ADD $2001, $2002
       MOVE $2003, $2001         ; fib_first = fib_temp
       INC $2000                 ; i++
       JMP _startfor             ; }
endfor
       PUSH $2002                ;  return fibnext
       RET
```

The Fibonacci function expressed in MOVE-based architecture:

```
fib    MOVE $0, $0
       MOVE index, $2000              ; (int index)
       MOVE &_basecase, eq_target     ;  index == 1
       MOVE #01, accumulator
       MOVE $2000, comparator
       MOVE &_basecase, eq_target     ; index == 2
       MOVE #02, accumulator
       MOVE $2000, comparator
       MOV &_startfib, program_counter
basecase
       MOVE #01,    $2002      ; return 1 or fib_next = 1
       MOVE &_endfor, program_counter
startfib
       MOVE #1,     $2001              ; fibfirst = 1
       MOVE #1,     $2002              ; fibnext  = 1
       MOVE #2,     $2004              ; i = 2

  _startfor MOVE &_endfor, ge_target ; i < index
       MOVE $2004, accumulator
       MOVE $2000, comparator

       MOVE $2002, $2003              ;fib_temp=fib_next
  ;fib_next=fib_next+fib_first
       MOVE $2001, accumulator
       MOVE $2002, adder
       MOVE accumulator, $2002
       MOVE $2003, $2001             ; fib_first = fib_temp
       MOVE #1, accumulator          ; i++
       MOVE $2000,  adder
       MOVE accumulator, $2000
       MOVE &_startfor, program_counter
endfor
       MOVE $2002, $(param_stack_ptr)   ;return fibnext
       MOVE #1, accumulator
       MOVE $param_stack_ptr,  adder
       MOVE accumulator, $param_stack_ptr
       MOVE $run_stack_ptr, $temp       ; RET
       MOVE #1, accumulator
       MOVE $run_stack_ptr, subtractor
       MOVE accumulator, $run_stack_ptr
       MOVE $temp, program_counter
```

9.3.2.4   Bubble Sort

The bubble sort is a simple but is also one of the least efficient sorting algorithms. The algorithm proceeds down the array, comparing and swapping the values into sorted order. This process continues until during a pass of the array, no exchanges of values take place. Values being sorted seem to "bubble" up to the correct location within the array. The bubble sort function takes a pointer to an array of integers and an integer size as its arguments.

The bubble sort algorithm in C is:

```c
#include <stdio.h>

void bsort(int list[], int size)
{
    int swapped;
    int x, temp;

    while(1)
    {
        swapped = 0;
        for(x = 0;x < size - 1;x++)
        {
            if(list[x] > list[x+1])
            {
                swapped    = 1;
                temp       = list[x];
                list[x]    = list[x+1];
                list[x+1]  = temp;
            }
        }

        if(0 == swapped)
            return;
    }
}
```

In generic assembly code:

```
_bsort      NOP
            MOVE &list, $1000    ;(int list[],
            MOVE size,  $1001    ;size)parameter passing

_while      MOVE #0, $1003       ; swapped = 0
            DEC $1001            ; size--
_for
            MOVE #0, $1004       ; x =0
            CMP $1004, $1001     ; x < size
            BGE _endfor
        ; compute list[x], list[x+1]
            LDA $1000            ; acc = &list[0]
            ADA $1004            ; acc = &list[0] + x
            STA $1005            ; temp1 = &list[x]
            MOVE $1005, $1006    ; temp2 = &list[x]
            INC $1006            ; temp2 = &list[x+1]
        ; compare array positions
            LDA $(1005)          ; acc = list[x]
            CMA $(1006)          ;if list[x] > list[x+1]
            BLE _endswap
        ; swap
            MOVE #1, $1003          ; swapped = 1
            MOVE $(1005), $1007     ; temp = list[x]
            MOVE $(1006), $(1005)   ; list[x] = list[x+1]
            MOVE $1007,   $(1006)   ; list[x+1] = temp
    endswap NOP

_endfor     JMP _for

            CMP #00, $1003       ; if swapped == 0
            BEQ _bsortend        ; return

_wend       JMP _while           ; while(1)
_bsortend RET                    ; return void from bsort
```

The Bubble sort algorithm expressed in MOVE-architecture is:

```
_bsort  MOVE $0, $0              ; nop
        MOVE &list, $1000        ;(int list[],
        MOVE size,  $1001        ; size) parameter passing

_while  MOVE #0, $1003           ; swapped = 0
        MOVE #1, accumulator     ; size--
        MOVE $1001, subtractor
        MOVE accumulator, $1001

_for    MOVE #0, $1004           ; x =0
        MOVE &_endfor, ge_target ; x < size
        MOVE $1004, accumulator
; compute list[x],list[x+1]
        MOVE $1001, comparator
        MOVE $1000, accumulator  ; acc = &list[0]
        MOVE $1004, adder        ; acc = &list[0] + x
        MOVE accumulator, $1005  ; temp1 = &list[x]
        MOVE $1005, $1006        ; temp2 = &list[x]
        MOVE #1, accumulator     ; temp2 = &list[x+1]
        MOVE $1006,  adder
    ; compare array positions
        MOVE accumulator, $1006
        MOVE $(1005), accumulator; acc = list[x]
        MOVE &_endswap, le-target  ; swap
   ; if list[x] > list[x+1]
        MOVE $(1006), comparator
        MOVE #1, $1003           ; swapped = 1
        MOVE $(1005), $1007      ; temp = list[x]
        MOVE $(1006), $(1005)    ; list[x] = list[x+1]
   ; list[x+1] = temp
endswap MOVE $0, $0
        MOVE $1007,    $(1006)

endfor  MOVE &_for, program_counter
        MOVE &_bsortend, eq_target ; return
        MOVE #00, accumulator      ; if swapped == 0
        MOVE $1003, comparator
wend    MOVE &_while, program_counter ; while(1)
bsortend MOVE $run_stack_ptr, $temp
    ;return void from bsort
        MOVE #1, accumulator
        MOVE $run_stack_ptr, subtractor
        MOVE accumulator, $run_stack_ptr
        MOVE $temp, program_counter
```

9.3.2.5 Greatest Common Denominator

The greatest common denominator (GCD) is the greatest positive integer that will evenly divide a pair of numbers. For example, the GCD of any two primes is always one. The Greek mathematician Euclid devised the clever, well-known GCD involving repeated modular division.

The C code for the function is:

```
#include <stdio.h>

int gcd(int a, int b)
{
    int r;

    while(b != 0)
    {
        r = a % b;
        a = b;
        b = r;
    }

    return a;
}
```

In generic assembly code:

```
gcd     NOP
        MOVE a, $3000         ;(int a
        MOVE b, $3001         ;int b) parameter pass by value
while   CMP #0, $3001         ;while(b != 0)
        BEQ _wend
                              ; {
        MOVE $3001, $3002     ; r = b
        MOD $3000, $3002      ; r = a mod r or r = a mod b
        MOVE $3001, $3000     ; a = b
        MOVE $3002, $3001     ; b = r
        JMP _while            ; }

Wend    PUSH $3000            ; return a
        RET
```

The greatest common denominator expressed in MOVE-based architecture is:

```
_gcd       MOVE $0, $0          ; NOP
           MOVE a, $3000        ;(int a
           MOVE b, $3001        ; int b) parameter pass by value

_while
           MOVE &_wend, eq_target      ;while(b != 0)
           MOVE #0, accumulator
           MOVE $3001, comparator
  ; {
           MOVE $3001, $3002        ; r = b
           MOD $3000, $3002      ; r = a mod r or r = a mod b
           MOVE $3001, $3000        ; a = b
           MOVE $3002, $3001        ; b = r
           MOVE &_while, program_counter   ; }
_wend      MOVE $3000, $(param_stack_ptr)    ; return a
           MOVE #1, accumulator
           MOVE $param_stack_ptr,   adder
           MOVE accumulator, $param_stack_ptr
           MOVE $run_stack_ptr, $temp        ; RET
           MOVE #1, accumulator
           MOVE $run_stack_ptr, subtractor
           MOVE accumulator, $run_stack_ptr
           MOVE $temp, program_counter
```

9.4   Implementing OISC using OISC

It is useful to show that there is a practical, as well as theoretical equivalence between the MOVE and SBN based OISC machines. In particular, such practical equivalence can assist in developing cross-assembling platforms that allow for the development of targeted assembly language code for either type of underlying architecture. In addition, while algorithms might be implemented in one OISC, it is convenient to be able to immediately map them into the other through the equivalence.

9.4.1   MOVE with SBN

The implementation of the AND instruction in SBN-based OISC illustrated that the MOVE instruction can be implemented with SBN. The synthesized instruction is:

```
MOVE operandam, operandum:

SBN operandum, #0x00000...0000, operandum, 0x0000000
```

By subtracting a constant zero from the operand, the result is a copy of the original operand.

9.4.2   SBN with MOVE

SBN can be synthesized with MOVE, although it requires several operations. Taking the form of SBN:

```
SBN operandam, operandum, resultant, next-address

NOT   operandum
ADD   operandam, operandum, resultant
ICMP  resultant, MAGIC_CONSTANT
BEQ   next-address
```

This breakdown of SBN indicates the need for a register to contain alternative target addresses for branches. Then the synthesized instruction is:

```
;MOVE operandum, #0xFFFFFFFF, XOR
  MOVE   operandam, 0x00000002
  MOVE   operandum, 0x0000FFFC
  MOVE 0x0000FFFC, resultant

;MOVE operandam, operandum,  ADD
  MOVE   operandam, 0x00000002
  MOVE   operandum, 0x0000FFFF
  MOVE 0x0000FFFF, resultant

;subtracted two operands, now compare
;MOVE next-address, branch target register
  MOVE next-address, 0x0000FA

;MOVE resultant, Comparator
  MOVE   #0x00000000, 0x00000002
  MOVE   resultant, 0x0000FFFE

;MOVE resultant to Status Register, trigger branch
  MOVE 0x0000FFFE, 0x00000001

;else continue sequentially if not negative
```

The constant zero is used for comparison against the result of the subtraction. If negative, the resulting bit string in the status register will trigger the branch, using the address in the branch target register. Another approach is to have a register that uses the appropriate branch-target register address (which is moved to the program counter) if the status changes.

9.5   Exercises

1. Which of the mappings from the standard types of computer architecture seem to map more easily than others? Why?

2. As a design approach, should the underlying hardware perform more functionality in one instruction, or should the software use less functionality and be synthesized with one instruction?

3. Regarding the mapping of high-level language statements to one instruction, is there a greatest lower bound on the size of the code with one instruction?

4. Implement a simple, well-known algorithm in conventional assembly for a processor, then implement it with one-instruction. Is the algorithm more or less difficult to implement?

5. For the algorithms that were implemented in this chapter, are any more suitable for one instruction than not? Is there a class of algorithms that are more suitable?

6. Implement a simple code fragment with MOVE and SBN. Compare the resulting assembly code. When does SBN seem better than MOVE? Is SBN just a more elaborate move instruction? Why or why not?

7. Map a computer's instruction set with one instruction. What conclusions from the instruction set can you make?

8. Can the instruction mappings of code generated for different computers from the same high-level language be used for an equitable comparison? Try it with the same high-level language algorithm or code fragment. Map the instruction set for a processor, and then map the generated assembly language from a high-level language compiler. Try this with several different processors.

9. For a computer of your choice implement a simple algorithm with one instruction, assuming that either SBN or MOVE are available. Then implement the same algorithm with the native instruction set. (Easily done if you compile the high-level language implementation.) What are the differences?

Chapter 10

PARALLEL ARCHITECTURES
Multiplicty

Great things are not done by impulse, but by a series of small things brought together.

Vincent Van Gogh (1853-1890), Dutch-born artist and one of the greatest of the Post-Impressionists who became a basic influence on the development of the Fauvism and Expressionism.

10.1   Von Neumann Bottleneck

For all its virtues, the stored-program computer paradigm contains a significant defect – the "von Neumann bottleneck." The bottleneck is caused by the fact that both data and instruction access uses the same bus, which has limited bandwidth. The processor, therefore, has to balance the number of instructions executed against the amount of data to be accessed. Furthermore, the stored program concept is inherently sequential, which does not work easily with the various parallel models of computation. High-speed memory internal and external to the processor, mitigates the problem, but also creates a cache coherence problem necessitating that the cache be kept in sync with main memory.

Both Hillis and Backus argue that processors are much faster than memory. By Moore's Law, the number of transistors on a microprocessor doubles approximately every 18 months. Thus the von Neumann bottleneck is exacerbated over time, limiting the possible gains in computational speed [Hillis98], [Backus78]. Also, unlike most high-level programming languages, the stored program concept does not distinguish instructions from data in memory. Hence there is a continuous stalemate between processor power and speed to slow memory.

10.2   Parallel Processing

It didn't take long for computer architects to identify the von Neumann bottleneck and attempt to mitigate it through various simultaneous or parallel processing schemes. The term "parallel computing" is varyingly used, but generally means computing different parts of the same problem simultaneously. In scientific computing, for example, it often means decomposing a problem into several sub-domains and computing a solution on each sub-domain separately and simultaneously.

One form of parallelism is trivial parallelism, sometimes called perfect parallelism. Many applications fall under the heading of trivial parallelism. These are applications in which one must compute many unrelated cases. That is, there is no parallelization of the algorithm or application; the code is subdivided among different processors, each working independently of the other.

Trivial parallelism requires that the serial code in different instances be mutually exclusive, hence readily subdivided. Some application domains that are considered trivially parallel are:

1. *Monte-Carlo methods* – these are problem solution approaches that involve random generation of feasible solutions and retention of the best.

2. *Cellular automata* – this is an alternative model of computation using a matrix configuration of processors whose behavior is some function of its eight neighbors.

3. *Matrix multiplication* – multiplying two compatible matrices.

One important metric of parallelism is speedup. Speedup can be stated as the sequential run time divided by parallel run time. Another more basic metric is the number of processors used by the parallel system, which sets a limit on the amount of parallelism that can be realized on the particular parallel computer.

One other parallel metric is the interconnection among the processors, measured in terms of number of connections for processors to communicate with one another. There are several different interconnection schemes. These include ring, mesh, or hypercube, amongst others (Fig. 10-1).

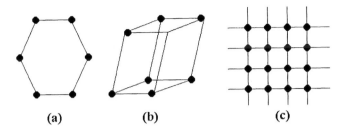

Figure 10-1. Three different multiprocessor interconnection schemes: (a) ring, (b) mesh, (c) hypercube.

10.2.1 Application Parallelism

Macroparallelism is parallelism at the application level, meaning the programmer must write the code with explicit parallelism in place. How an application is parallelized can impact how well it scales to solve a problem.

There are two parallel laws, the first was stated in 1967 by Gene Amdahl, and widely cited thereafter. The second, by Gustafson in the late 1980s evaluated the underlying basis of Amdahl's Law and showed it did not hold empirically.

10.2.1.1 Amdahl's Law

Amdahl's Law is a statement regarding the level of parallelization that can be achieved by a parallel computer. Amdahl's law states that for a constant problem size, speedup approaches zero as the number of processor elements grows. It expresses a bound of parallelism in terms of speedup as a property of software, not a hardware limit.

Formally, let n be the number of processors available for parallel processing. Let s be fraction of the code that is of a serial nature only, that is, it cannot be parallelized. A simple reason why a portion of code cannot be parallelized would be a sequence of operations, each depending on the result off the previous operation. Clearly $(1-s)$ is the fraction of code that can be parallelized. The speedup is then given as the ratio of the code before allocation to the parallel processors to the ratio of that afterwards. That is

$$\text{speedup} = \frac{s + (1-s)}{\left(s + \dfrac{(1-s)}{n}\right)}$$

$$= \frac{1}{\left(s + \dfrac{(1-s)}{n}\right)}$$

$$= \frac{1}{\left(\dfrac{ns}{n} + \dfrac{(1-s)}{n}\right)}$$

$$= \frac{1}{\left(\dfrac{ns + 1 - s}{n}\right)}$$

$$= \frac{n}{ns + 1 - s}$$

Hence,

$$\text{speedup} = \frac{n}{1 + (n-1)s} \qquad (10\text{-}1)$$

Clearly for $s = 0$ linear speedup as a function of the number of processors can be obtained. But for $s > 0$ perfect speedup is not possible due to the sequential component.

Amdahl's Law is frequently cited as an argument against parallel systems and massively parallel processors. Of Amdahl's Law, Hillis states "there will always be a part of the computation which is inherently sequential, no matter how much you speed up the remaining 90 percent, the computation as a whole will never speed up by more than a factor of 10. The processors working on the 90 percent that can be done in parallel will end up waiting for the single processor to finish the sequential 10 percent of the task" [Hillis98].

But the argument is flawed. One underlying assumption of Amdahl's law is that the problem size is constant, and then at some point there is a diminishing margin of return for speeding up the computation. Problem sizes, however, tend to scale with the size of a parallel system. Bigger parallel systems in number of processors are used to solve very big problems in science and mathematics.

Amdahl's Law stymied the field of parallel and massively parallel computers, creating an insoluble problem that limited the efficiency and application of parallelism to different problems. The skeptics of parallelism took Amdahl's Law as the insurmountable bottleneck to any kind of practical parallelism. However, later research provided new insights into Amdahl's Law and its relation to parallelism.

10.2.1.2 Gustafson's Law

Gustafson demonstrated with a 1024-processor system that the basic presumptions in Amdahl's Law are inappropriate for massive parallelism [Gustafson88]. Gustafson found that the underlying principle that "the problem size scales with the number of processors, or with a more powerful processor, the problem expands to make use of the increased facilities is inappropriate" [Gustafson88].

Gustafson's empirical results demonstrated that the parallel or vector part of a program scales with the problem size. Times for vector start-up, program loading, serial bottlenecks, and I/O that make up the serial component of the run do not grow with the problem size [Gustafson88].

Gustafson formulated that if the serial time, s and parallel time $p = (1 - s)$ on a parallel system with n processors, then a serial processor would require the time:

$$s + p \cdot n \tag{10-2}$$

Comparing the plots of equations 10-1 and 10-2 in Fig. 10-2, it can be seen that Gustafson presents a much more optimistic picture of speedup due to parallelism than does Amdahl.

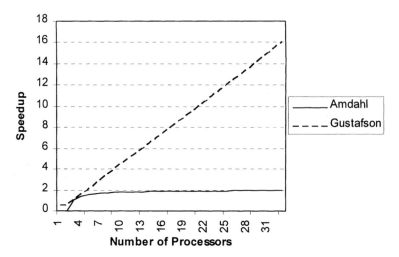

Figure 10-2. Linear speedup of Gustafson compared to "diminishing return" speedup of Amdahl with 50% of code available for parallelization. Notice as number of processors increase speedup does not increase indefinitely for Amdahl due to serial component.

Unlike the curve for Amdahl's Law, Gustafson's Law is a simple line. Gustafson goes on to state, "one with a much more moderate slope: $1 - n$. It is thus much easier to achieve parallel performance than is implied by Amdahl's paradigm."

Hillis gives a different discussion on the flaw of Amdahl's Law, in which he states, "a more efficient way to use a parallel computer is to have each processor perform similar work, but on a different section of the data...where large computations are concerned this method works surprisingly well." [Hillis98] Doing the same task but on a different range of data circumvents an underlying presumption in Amdahl's Law, as Hillis puts it: "the assumption that a fixed portion of the computation...must be sequential. This estimate sounds plausible, but it turns out not to be true of most computations." In essence, Hillis without technical jargon, states Gustafson's Law.

10.2.2   Macroparallelism : Parallelization of Quicksort Algorithm

C.A.R. Hoare discovered the Quicksort algorithm, which is considered one of the fastest sorting algorithms on a serial machine, with a linearithmic theoretical least upper bound of $O(n \cdot \log n)$ for a data set size n [Hoare62]. The Quicksort algorithm, however, degenerates into a quadratic complexity of $O(n^2)$ for the worst case of an already sorted sequence of elements.

The mechanics of the operation of the Quicksort algorithm have been thoroughly analyzed and documented, but how the Quicksort is parallelized from a recursive serial algorithm illustrates the non-trivial parallelism. Parallelization for the Quicksort with a parallel system of *m* processors would theoretically reduce the time to $O(n \log n)/m$.

The Quicksort algorithm works by partitioning the array to be sorted, then recursively sorting each partition. In the partitioning process one of the array elements is selected as a pivot value. Values smaller than the pivot values are placed to the left of the pivot, while larger values are placed to the right. The array list of elements, once partitioned with a pivot value, is a set of independent sub-lists. Each sub-list can be partitioned in the same manner, until the sub-list is one element, at which point the array list is sorted.

Quicksort is a divide-and-conquer algorithm that sorts a sequence by recursively dividing it into smaller sub-sequences. To parallelize, sorting the smaller sub-lists represents two completely independent sub-problems that can be solved independently in parallel.

One possible way to parallelize Quicksort is to run it initially on a single processor as the serial algorithm would. Once the algorithm performs the pivoting for recursive partitioning, assign one of the sub-lists to another processor. Each processor then partitions its array by using Quicksort, and assigning one of its sub-lists to another processor. The algorithm completes when the sub-lists cannot be further partitioned. The parallelization takes advantage of the mutual exclusion of the pivoting and recursive recurrence relation among the generated sub-lists.

10.2.3   Instruction-level Parallelism

Microparallelism or instruction-level parallelism is implicit parallelism within the machine code of an application. Microparallelism is possible on a serial machine; the actual parallelization is within the processor on the instruction stream. While microparallelism is transparent and implicit to the application, even on a serial computer, the computer processor and instruction set must support it. The application compiler, which translates the high-level C and FORTRAN source code into machine code, must generate code that takes advantage of the possibility for micro parallelism.

There are two categories of microparallelism:

1. implicit – within the microprocessor and transparent to the compiler, and

2. explicit – parallelism that the compiler can exploit, yielding "true" parallelism.

Internal or implicit parallelism within the processor is independent of the high-level application compiler, the sequence of instructions are pipelined. A compiler can optimize code to avoid pipeline hazards to maintain a queue of instructions in the pipeline.

10.2.3.1 Implicit Microparallelism

Pipelining is implicit parallelism in the different cycles of processing an instruction. Most instructions have a instruction cycle of:

1. fetch – get the instruction from memory,
2. decode – determine what the instruction is,
3. execute – perform the instruction decode, and
4. write – store the results to memory.

Non-pipelined, one instruction processed through a cycle at a time is scalar execution. With pipelining, more instructions can be processed in different cycles simultaneously, improving processor performance.

For example, consider Fig. 10-3. The first picture shows the sequential (scalar) execution of the fetch, decode, execute, and write components of three instructions. The sequence requires twelve clock cycles. Beneath the sequence is shown another set of the same three instructions, plus eight more instructions, with overlapping execution of the components. The first three instructions are completed in only six clock cycles and most of the remaining instructions are completed within the twelve clock cycles.

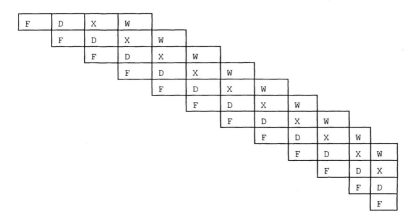

Figure 10-3. Sequential instruction execution versus pipelined instruction execution.

One disadvantage of pipelining is that it can actually degrade performance. Pipelining is a form of predictive execution in that the instructions that are prefetched are taken to be the next sequential instructions. If any of the instructions in the pipeline are a branch instruction, the prefetched instructions are no longer valid. In this case, the pipeline registers and flags must all be reset – i.e. the pipeline is flushed, which takes time. Pipelining will improve overall performance when code execution tends to be more sequential than not. Otherwise, it may degrade performance.

Pipelining does not provide as much of an advantage in one instruction computing because each instruction is very primitive, and therefore not greatly decomposed. For example, the MOVE as a one instruction has the cycle of:

1. execute – perform the instruction decoded, and
2. write – store the results to memory.

The fetch and decode are unnecessary, as there is only one instruction. Hence, minimal overlapping of instructions can occur.

In Fig. 10-4 a sequential execution of three complex instructions is compared to the sequential execution of a one instruction computer, and the pipelined instruction execution for the one instruction.

Sequential instruction execution

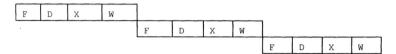

Sequential one instruction execution

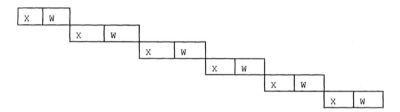

Pipelined one instruction execution

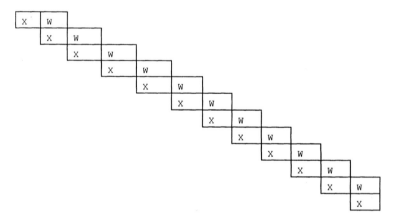

Figure 10-4. Sequential instruction execution of a complex instruction as compared to sequential instruction execution for a simple one instruction computer and pipelined instruction execution for the one instruction computer.

The MOVE one instruction can execute more cycles in scalar execution than the non-OISC (either a CISC or RISC instruction). For the three scalar instructions executed, the OISC executes six, twice as many for the given timeframe.

When pipelined, all but one of the OISC instructions is complete in the same timeframe. Eleven OISC instructions execute for three non-OISC instructions in scalar form. The pipelined non-OISC has nine instructions complete, with three in the various cycles of the instruction.

A comparison of the number of instructions that can be completed in the same 12 clock cycles is given in Table 10-1. Clearly the pipelined OISC offers the best performance with 11 instructions completed as opposed to nine for the non-OISC computer.

Table 10-1. Comparing number of instructions either completely or partially executed during the same twelve clock cycles in a sequential and pipelined configurations for one instruction and non-one instruction (complex) computers.

	One instruction	Complex instruction
Sequential	6	3
Pipelined Complete	11	9
Pipelined Incomplete	1	3

OISC pipelining has another advantage in reducing program size in memory, offsetting the increase in size when implemented as MOVE-accumulator.

10.2.3.2 Explicit Microparallelism

The other microparallelism is explicit. In effect, the generated machine code is optimized by the compiler to increase the amount of parallelism in the instructions and decrease instruction-to-instruction coupling. The MOVE instruction using the accumulator can use microparallelism. Consider the following C program that implements an average function.

```c
int avg(int list[], int size)
{
    int x, sum;
    sum = 0;

  for(x=0; x < size; x++)
    {
        sum += list[x];
    }
        return (sum / size);
}
```

The code can be "compiled" to a corresponding program using MOVE OISC as follows:

```
avg       MOVE $0,$0                      ; nop
          MOVE &list,$1000                ; avg(list[], size)
          MOVE size,$1001
          MOVE #00,$1002                  ; sum = 0
          MOVE #00,$1003                  ; x = 0
for       MOVE &_endfor, ge_target        ; branch >= _endfor
          MOVE $1001,accumulator          ; x < size
          MOVE $1003,comparator
          MOVE $1000,accumulator          ; acc = &list
          MOVE $1003,adder                ; acc = acc + x
          MOVE accumulator,$1004          ; temp = &list[x]
          MOVE $(1004),accumulator        ; acc  = list[x]
          MOVE $1002,adder                ; acc  = acc + sum
          MOVE accumulator,$1002          ; sum  = acc
          MOVE #01,accumulator            ; x++
          MOVE $1003,adder
          MOVE accumulator,adder
          MOVE &_for,program_counter      ; }
endfor    MOVE $1001,accumulator          ; sum = sum / size
          MOVE $1002,divider
          MOVE accumulator,$1002          ; sum on return stack
          MOVE $1002,$(param_stack_p
          MOVE #01, accumulator
          MOVE $param_stack_ptr, add
          MOVE accumulator, $param_s
          MOVE $run_stack_ptr, $temp      ; return
          MOVE #1, accumulator
          MOVE $run_stack_ptr, subtr
          MOVE accumulator, $run_sta
          MOVE $temp, program_counte
```

The microparallelization of the sequence of MOVE instructions requires that the operands for each MOVE be mutually exclusive. Essentially all the operands in the block are unique, with no duplicates.

Dividing the code into mutually exclusive parallel segments creates a shorter program of parallelized segments.

```
avg      MOVE $0, $0                              ;nop
         MOVE &list,$1000                         ;avg(list[],size)
         MOVE size,$1001
         MOVE #00,$1002                           ; sum = 0
         MOVE #00,$1003                           ; x = 0
for      MOVE &_endfor,ge_target                  ;branch >=endfor
         MOVE $1001,accumulator                   ;x < size
         MOVE $1003,comparator
         MOVE $1000,accumulator                   ;acc = &list
         MOVE $1003,adder                         ;acc = acc + x
         MOVE accumulator,$1004                   ;temp =&list[x]
         MOVE $(1004),accumulator                 ;acc  = list[x]

         MOVE $1002,adder                         ;acc =acc+sum
         MOVE accumulator,$1002                   ;sum  = acc
         MOVE #01,accumulator                     ;x++
         MOVE $1003,adder
         MOVE accumulator,adder                   ; }
         MOVE &_for,program_counter
endfor   MOVE $1001,accumulator                   ;sum=sum/size
         MOVE $1002,divider
         MOVE accumulator,$1002                   ;sum on return
         MOVE$1002, $(param_stack_ptr)            ;stack
         MOVE #01,accumulator
         MOVE $param_stack_ptr, adder
         MOVE accumulator,$param_stack            ; return
         MOVE $run_stack_ptr, $temp
         MOVE #1, accumulator
         MOVE$run_stack_ptr,subtractor
         MOVEaccumulator,$run_stack_pt
         MOVE $temp, program_counter
```

The MOVE-accumulator assembly code shortens into 17-lines of parallelized code. Not all the MOVE instructions could be parallelized, having a coupling in several sequences of instructions with the accumulator register, or a memory address.

The end result is that there are seventeen parallel segments, which theoretically can be executed simultaneously. However, hardware constraints such as the data bus, internal data path conflicts, and so on can limit how much parallelism can be utilized.

10.2.4   Information Interchange

The major difference between two parallel systems is the means for which data is exchanged and interchanged between processors. The two mechanisms for data interchange are:

1. message passing, and
2. shared memory.

Message passing involves exchanging discrete messages between processors. The message passing interface (MPI) is a common software package used for messaging. All information exchanged among the processors is uniform, a message is a message. Message passing is a software-oriented approach to parallelism, in that the actual processors may be distributed across a network.

Shared memory among the processors is a hardware-oriented solution. Shared memory uses a model where each processor can address another processor as memory. This is a non-uniform means of interchanging data, as memory for a processor is different from memory to a shared memory space, to memory which are the other processor registers. Shared memory is often organized into different configurations, such as interleaved or distributed memory. The programmable random access machine (PRAM) is the general form used for shared memory parallel systems.

10.3   Flynn's Taxonomy for Parallelism

The generally accepted taxonomy of parallel systems was developed by Flynn [Flynn66]. The classification is based on the notion of two streams of information flow to a processor, instructions and data. These two streams can be either single or multiple, giving four classes of machines:

1. single instruction single data (SISD),
2. single instruction multiple data (SIMD),
3. multiple instruction single data (MISD),
4. multiple instruction multiple data (MIMD).

Table 10-2 shows the four primary classes and some of the architectures that fit in those class. Most of these architectures have either been discussed or will be discussed shortly.

Table 10-2. Classification for Computer Architectures

	single data stream	multiple data stream
single instruction stream	von neumann processors RISC	systolic processors wavefront processors
multiple instruction stream	pipelined architectures VLIW processors	dataflow processors transputers grid computers hypercube processors

10.3.1   Single Instruction Single Data (SISD)

The single instruction single data (SISD) architectures encompass standard serial von Neumann architecture computers. In a sense, the SISD category is the base metric for Flynn's taxonomy.

There are a number of ways to introduce parallelism into the architecture of serial computers, such as microparallelism and using multiple functional units within the processor. Another possibility is to overlap processor operations with input-output, letting the processor concurrently execute instructions during I/O operations.

10.3.1.1 Single Instruction Multiple Data (SIMD)

The single instruction multiple data (SIMD) computers are essentially array processors. This type of parallel computer architecture has n-processors, each executing the same instruction, but on different data streams. Often each element in the array can only communicate with its nearest neighbor, this design feature limits the classes of problems that can be processed.

An array or SIMD machine is often used for such computation as processing a matrix. Other problem categories include particle physics, modeling air and fluid flow, and weather forecasting. SIMD machines were among the first parallel computer architectures that were implemented, supporting many data streams simultaneously being an extension of serial computers.

A pipelined computer, such as a Cray I, could be viewed as a SIMD machine, each pipeline operates independently as a data stream, but all of the pipelines execute under the control of an instruction processor. Several array processor SIMD-style parallel computers were constructed in the late 1960s and early 1970s.

Another example, SOLOMON, was a parallel array computer with 1024 processor elements arranged in a grid. The SOLOMON computer was never built, but served as the impetus for other architectures including the Illiac IV machine.

10.3.2   Multiple Instruction Single Data (MISD)

The multiple instruction single data (MISD) classification in Flynn's taxonomy is a theoretical parallel computer architecture that lends itself naturally to those computations requiring an input to be subjected to several operations, each receiving the input in its original form. These applications include classification problems and digital signal processing. In a sense, the MISD category exists more for completeness of the taxonomy created by Flynn, than for reflecting an actual kind of parallel computer architecture in use. Nevertheless, pipelined and very long instruction word architectures are usually considered in this class.

In pipelined architectures, for example, more than one instruction can be processed simultaneously (one for each level of pipeline). However, since only one instruction can use data at any one time, it is considered MISD.

Similarly, VLIW computers tend to be implemented with microinstructions that have very long bit-lengths (and hence more capability). Hence, rather than breaking down macroinstructions into numerous microinstructions, several (nonconflicting) macroinstructions can be combined into several microinstructions. For example, if object code was generated that loaded one register followed by an increment of another register, these two instructions could be executed simultaneously by the processor (or at least appear so at the macroinstruction level) with a series of long microinstructions.   Since only nonconflicting instructions can be combined, any two accessing the data bus cannot. Therefore the very long instruction word computer is MISD.

One "real" implementation of MISD, is Carnegie-Mellon's Hydra/Computer multi-mini-processor project or C.mmp in 1971. The architecture was not an explicit MISD, but supported MISD operation. [Bell82].

10.3.3   Single Instruction Multiple Data (SIMD)

Computer architectures that are usually classified as SIMD are systolic and wavefront array parallel computers. In both systolic and wavefront processors, each processing element is executing the same (and only) instruction but on different data. Hence these architectures are SIMD.

10.3.3.1 Systolic Processors

Systolic processors consist of a large number of uniform processors connected in an array topology. Each processor usually performs only one specialized operation and has only enough local memory to perform its designated operation, and to store the inputs and outputs. Hence, they are one instruction set computers.

The individual processors, called processing elements, take inputs from the top and left, perform a specified operation, and output the results to the right and bottom. One such processing element is depicted in Fig. 10-5. The processors are connected to the four nearest neighboring processors in the nearest neighbor topology .

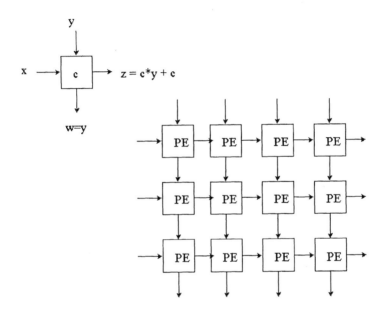

Figure 10-5. A systolic computer showing basic processing element (PE) and mesh configuration of multiple elements. A systolic computer is truly a OISC because each processing element can perform only one operation.

Processing or firing at each of the cells occurs simultaneously in synchronization with a central clock. The fact that each cell fires on this heartbeat lends the name systolic. Inputs to the system are from memory stores or input devices at the boundary cells at the left and top. Outputs to memory or output devices are obtained from boundary cells at the right and bottom.

Systolic processors are fast and can be implemented in VLSI. They are somewhat troublesome, however, in dealing with propagation delays in the connection buses and in the availability of inputs when the clock ticks.

10.3.3.2 Wavefront Processor

Wavefront processors consist of an array of identical processors, each with its own local memory and connected in a nearest neighbor topology. Each processor usually performs only one specialized operation. Hybrids containing two or more different type cells are possible. The cells fire asynchronously when all required inputs from the left and top are present. Outputs then appear to the right and below. Unlike the systolic processor, the outputs are the unaltered inputs. That is, the top input is transmitted unaltered to the bottom output bus, and the left input is transmitted, unaltered, to the right output bus. Also, different from the systolic processor, outputs from the wavefront processor are read directly from the local memory of selected cells and output obtained form boundary cells. Inputs are still placed on the top and left input buses of boundary cells. The fact that inputs propagate through the array unaltered like a wave gives this architecture its name.

Wavefront processors combine the best of systolic architectures with dataflow architectures. That is, they support an asynchronous dataflow computing structure –timing in the interconnection buses and at input and output devices is not a problem. Furthermore, the structure can be implemented in VLSI.

10.3.4   Multiple Instruction Multiple Data (MIMD)

Multiple instruction multiple data (MIMD) computers involve large numbers of processors that are capable of executing more than one instruction and on more than one datum at any instant in time. Except for networks of distributed multiprocessors working on the same problem (grid computing) these are "exotic" architectures. Two paradigms that follow MIMD are dataflow computers and transputers.

10.3.4.1 Dataflow Architectures

Dataflow architectures use a large number of special processors in a topology in which each of the processors is connected to every other. Each of the processors has its own local memory and a counter. Special tokens are passed between the processors asynchronously. These tokens, called activity packets, contain an opcode, operand count, operands, and list of destination addresses for the result of the computation. An example of a generic activity packet is given in Fig. 10-6. Each processor's local memory is used to hold a list of activity packets for that processor, the operands needed for the current activity packet, and a counter used to keep track of the number of operands received. When the number of operands stored in local memory is equivalent to that required for the operation in the current activity packet, the operation is performed and the results are sent to the specified destinations. Once an activity packet has been executed, the processor begins working on the next activity packet in its execution list.

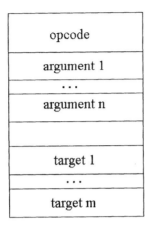

Figure 10-6. Generic activity template for dataflow machine.

Dataflow architectures are an excellent parallel solution for signal processing, but require a cumbersome graphical programming language.

10.3.4.2 Transputers

Transputers are fully self-sufficient, multiple instruction set, von Neumann processors. The instruction set includes directives to send data or receive data via ports that are connected to other transputers. The transputers, though capable of acting as a uniprocesor, are best utilized when connected in a nearest neighbor configuration. In a sense, the transputer provides a wavefront or systolic processing capability but without the restriction of a single instruction. Indeed, by providing each transputer in a network with an appropriate stream of data and synchronization signals, wavefront or systolic computers—which can change configurations—can be implemented.

Transputers have been widely used in embedded real-time applications, and commercial implementations are readily available. Moreover, tool support, such as the multitasking language occam-2, has made it easier to build transputer-based applications.

10.4   Exercises

1. Is general-purpose parallel computation possible with one instruction? Why or why not?

2. Take a problem for a specific parallel architecture such as hypercube, systolic, wavefront, and attempt to re-write it in terms of one instruction. What are the difficulties in the porting process?

3. How do shared memory and message passing differ from the one-instruction parallel implementation of a program? Would the reverse, taking the implementation of a one-instruction parallel problem, be easily rewritten in shared memory or message passing?

4. Do some of the parallel computation problems couple with a particular hardware organization? For a particular problem on a parallel machine, can one instruction parallelism be used within the constraints of the hardware architecture?

Chapter 11

APPLICATIONS AND IMPLEMENTATIONS
And the Future

What is now proved was once only imagined.

William Blake (1757-1827), English romantic poet, printmaker, painter, and engraver.

11.1 "OISC-like" Phenomena

One instruction computing is based on the principle of taking one behavior and repeatedly applying it to create more complex behaviors. This phenomenon is not confined to OISC. Other examples exist in nature and in other domains.

11.1.1 Transistors in Integrated Circuits

All integrated circuits (ICs) are constructed from the fundamental component of a transistor. From transistors other circuit elements can be synthesized, such as digital logic gates, amplifiers, and other electronic components.

Since only one element is used, these elements can be reduced to very large-scale integrated (VLSI) circuits. The amount of miniaturization that has been realized since the introduction of the IC in the late 1950s is due to the redundancy and simplicity of the one component.

11.1.2 NAND/NOR Gate Logic

In digital logic, the NAND gate, and NOR gate have a universal property which allows all other logic gates to be constructed from NAND or NOR gates. The AND, OR, XOR, and NOT gates, however, can be constructed from NAND and NOR gates in different combinations.

The more complex logic circuits formed from the basic logic gates such as multiplexers and decoders can likewise be synthesized from NOR and NAND logic gates. This is the basic principle from which the half adder architecture evolved.

11.1.3   Biological Cells and DNA

All living cells are essentially alike. The simplest life forms are one-celled bacteria, which are the likely progenitors of more complex life. Cells differentiate themselves and specialize based on the genetic code in the deoxyribonucleic acid (DNA). But since each cell contains the DNA of the organism, they are alike.

This simplicity allows for the complex biological organization of a living organism. Growth, repair of damaged tissue, and adaptation of organs and tissues is facilitated by the simplicity of the cell.

Metaphors of nature are often made in computation. For example, the brain is often likened to a neural network, and evolution to a genetic algorithm. Therefore, finding a single scalable mechanism in nature is likewise possible to have a similar metaphor in computation. Such a metaphor would open up alternatives to the classic "hard problems" of computation, and new perspectives on the basic nature of computation. In this context, using DNA and cellular computing seems to be a natural match. Theoretical implementation of a cellular computer is discussed later in this chapter.

11.1.4   Fractals

While there is a formal, mathematical definition of a fractal involving metrics spaces, a more informal definition is that it is an infinitely self-similar object. Really, a fractal is a dynamical system that has to be formalized for a proper discussion, which is out of the scope of the text. However, it is the self-similarity of the fractals that is reminiscent of OISC and is, therefore, of interest.

There are several ways to generate fractals, including through random number generation, calculation of escaping (non-convergent) points, and iteration of some simple operation. It is the latter method that is most OISC-like.

To illustrate briefly, consider an operation performed on a triangle in which it is sub-divided into three congruent triangles. These in turn are similarly sub-divided and so on. After sufficient repeated application of the operation, an image of arbitrary self-similarity can be generated. This object is well known as the Sierpinski Triangle (Fig. 11-1).

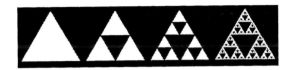

Figure 11-1. Evolution of the Sierpinski Triangle. The image is obtained in a number of ways including through the repetitive application of a simple rule (four steps, moving left to right, shown). A certain cellular automaton can also generate the image.

Fractals are found in a number of applications areas including image compression. They have become somewhat more of a curiosity, however, than the revolutionary mathematical tool that they were once thought to be.

11.1.5 Cellular Automata

Cellular automata, which were originally investigated by von Neumann, consist of a space of unit cells. These cells are initialized with some value, usually a "1" representing a live cell (with "0" representing a dead or unoccupied cell). Other characterizations for the contents of the cells can be made, but each cell behaves according to the same, basic rule. The rule describes the contents of a unit cell at time t in terms of the contents of the cell and its neighbors at time $t-1$. In a sense, each cell behaves like a one instruction computer. Collectively, the behavior of these cells over time, can express complex behavior. Cellular automata can exhibit chaotic (unpredictable) behavior or they can converge to a steady state or even tend to some kind of periodic behavior.

Cellular automata have been widely studied, but there seems to be little practical use for them other then to model certain interesting theoretical behaviors.

11.2 Field Programmable Gate Arrays

In looking for a practical platform for implementing a processor based on one instruction it is natural to consider the field programmable gate arrays (FPGA). FPGAs have reached usable densities in the hundreds of thousands of gates and flip-flops that can be integrated to form system level solutions. Clock structures can be driven using dedicated clocks that are provided within the system. FPGAs are infinitely reprogrammable (even within the system) and design modifications can be made quickly and easily [Xilinx98]. Hence, they are well adapted to the massed digital logic approach of OISC.

In an FPGA, the programmable logic consists of a series of logic blocks (LB) connected in either segmented or continuous interconnect structures (Fig. 11-2). Segmented interconnections are used for short signals between adjacent configurable logic blocks (CLB), while continuous interconnections are used for bus-structured architectures [Xilinx98].

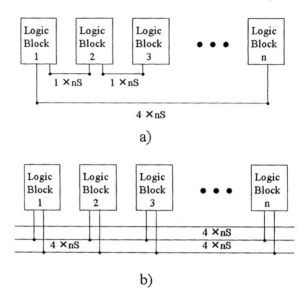

Figure 11-2. Segmented (a) and continuous (b) interconnection strategies for FPGA logic blocks [Xilinx98].

Each logic block uses one or more look up table (LUT) and several bits of memory. The contents of the LUTs are reprogrammable by changing the contents of the LUTs. I/O blocks are usually connected to local memories. This design allows for maximum flexibility, and FPGAs can be used to implement circuit diagrams into the logic blocks (Fig. 11-3). The logic blocks can be configured to exploit parallelism.

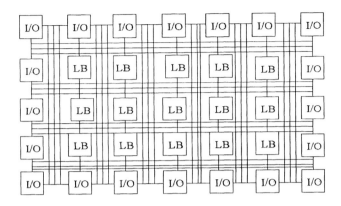

Figure 11-3. A conceptual illustration of an FPGA showing internal configurable logic blocks and periphery I/O elements.

The continuous structure is ideal for connecting large numbers of simple logic units, such as half adders, full adders and twos complement inverters. Each of these can easily be constructed from a single logical operation [Laplante90]. Moreover, these logic blocks can also be pre-designed to implement higher-level functions, such as vector addition, convolution, or even an FFT. The ability to reconfigure logic blocks gives the flexibility to select a single instruction and use it to implement the necessary functionality. This is a key strength of an FPGA solution to implementing a OISC.

Implementation of memory decoders, DMA, clocks etc. are straightforward because the FPGA manufacturers provide these as core logic elements. Indeed since all the basic logic functions have been provided, realization of any standard computer hardware is just an exercise in patience and large-scale integration. Since each HA is a simple CLB interconnected in continuous fashion, the half adder architecture is perhaps the closest to existing logic implementations using FPGAs.

Two major FPGA manufacturers, Altera and Xilinx, provide designs for configuring their FPGAs as a microprocessor, or soft processor. Altera's offering is called Nios®, Xilinx's is called MicroBlaze®. Both designs demonstrate how a more complex instruction set computer can be implemented – presumably making implementation of a one instruction computer far simpler.

At the moment FPGAs are desirable for implementing any OISC solution because they are inexpensive and can be reconfigured to implement the fundamental instruction. Moreover, there exists a rich toolset to develop applications for FPGAs including high order language compilers, simulators, and logic minimization software.

11.2.1   Development Environment

A rich development environment is available for producing CLBs for standard commercial FPGAs. Fig. 11-4 (a) illustrates the traditional development cycle of Verilog/VHSIC Hardware Description Language (VHDL) programming to produce FPGA Net lists. Fig. 11-4 (b) illustrates the software support tools needed for a OISC system. The high order language compiler takes source code, typically in a language very close to C and converts it to OISC symbolic code. The OISC compiler converts the symbolic code either directly into native instructions for the machine, or into Verilog or VHDL. The purpose of the alternate compilation path is to permit simulation of the code on FPGA simulators, or for direct mapping to an FPGA.

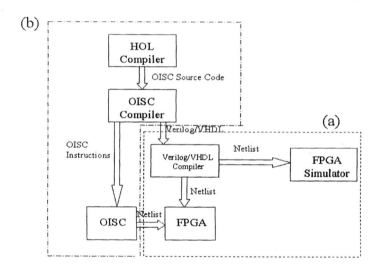

Figure 11-4. Mapping OISC into VHDL then to an FPGA. (a) represents the existing software support. (b) represents new support tools needed for OISC.

For example, in the case of the Xilinx FPGA, code targeted for a C compiler called Handel-C® is complied into a Xilinx netlist before place and route, pin allocation and creation of FPGA configuration bitstream file [Xilinx98]. Handel-C® is similar to ANSI C except that the former provides language constructs for forcing parallelization of operations. The Handel-C© simulator enables simulation of the system for rapid prototyping and debugging. Many predefined routines exist for fasting system development.

Verilog is a popular language used in synthesizing designs for FPGAs. While it is less verbose than traditional VHDL and is now being standardized by the IEEE 1364 working group, it was not originally intended as an input to synthesis since many Verilog constructs are not supported by synthesis software [Xilinx97].

VHDL is a hardware description language used for designing integrated circuits. Like Verilog, it was not intended for synthesis. However, the high level abstraction of VHDL makes it easier to describe system components that are not synthesized [Xilinx97]. Another advantage of using standard languages like VHDL and Verilog is that gate reduction can be realized through the use of a commercial tool, such as Synopsys' DesignWare®.

Because of standardization, implementations are portable across commercial FPGA types and further expand the set of available CLBs. Table 11-1 shows the applicable standards for VHDL, Verilog and for the Std_logic data type used in programming the FPGA using version of standard ANSI C.

Table 11-1. Industry standards for FPGA programming .

Standard	Version
VHDL Language	IEEE-STD-1076-87
Verilog Language	IEEE-STD-1364-95
Std_logic Data Type	IEEE-STD-1164-93

11.3   Applications

One instruction computers are largely a curiosity. There are, however, a number of problems that fit well with the PISC paradigm. Two of these are discussed in great detail to illustrate the potential utility of OISC.

11.3.1   Genetic Algorithm

The OISC computer architecture with its generality and simplicity makes implementing a genetic algorithm processor or engine not only possible, but also architecturally appropriate. In effect, the functionality of the genetic algorithm operators becomes memory addresses – the genetic algorithm operators implemented in hardware. The organization of the memory addresses creates virtual registers, which are used to implement the algorithm. The genetic algorithm itself is based on a MOVE architecture. Fig. 11-5 illustrates the architecture for a MOVE-based Genetic Algorithm processor.

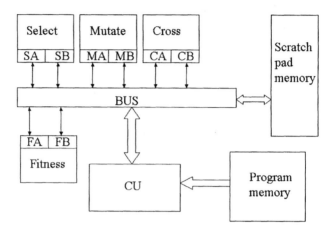

Figure 11-5. An architecture for a MOVE-based OISC for a Genetic Algorithm [Laplante03].

The crux of the processor is the implementation of the Genetic Algorithm operators. The remaining instructions can be synthesized to provide ancillary support.

The following sections describe much of the detailed implementation of the Genetic Algorithm using MOVE-based OISC. While a simulator has been built and tested (see Appendix A) only the necessary C-code and MOVE-based OISC equivalent to illustrate the feasibility of the approach. The MOVE-based OISC code is indented and preceded by the mnemonic "asm" for readability. In addition, most of the prologue, epilogue, and variable declarations are omitted for brevity.

11.3.1.1 Chromosome Design

Each chromosome is a binary word in memory where each binary substring is assigned to one of the variables in the problem to be optimized. For instance, 128 bits will be used in the running example to represent two 64-bit variables. When the algorithm completes, the chromosome can be decoded back to the problem parameters.

The C declaration for the chromosome is given below and is provided to increase the readability of subsequent C code and its MOVE-based OISC equivalent.

```
/* sizeof chromosome is 2 64-bit words or 16-bytes */
 typedef struct
   {
     float fitness;   /* 64-bit float */
     long  gene;      /* 64-bit long  */
   } chromosome;      /* end chromosome */
```

Naturally, in a real OISC computer the allocation of the data structures needs to be taken care of manually. But in the case of using FPGAs, the translation software takes care of this (and is described later).

The chromosome population is initialized using a simple looping construct and random number generator.

11.3.1.2 Objective or Fitness Function

The objective or fitness function is represented as two memory addresses, one for the chromosome (address FA in Fig. 11-5), and another for the fitness value (address FB). After moving a chromosome into the fitness register, the fitness value is generated and placed in the fitness value register. In a 64-bit word system, the fitness value can be a floating-point value between 0.0 and 1.0.

The equivalent C code and MOVE-based OISC for the fitness function is:

```
#define MUTATION_RATE 0.01
#define PASSTHRU_RATE 0.05

 void eval_fitness(chromosome *c)
 {
     asm Move c->gene, FITNESS_REG;
     asm Move FITNESS_REG, c->fitness;

 }/* end fitness */
```

11.3.1.3 Selection

Selection is implemented with two memory addresses that act as registers. The first (address SA in Fig. 11-5) is the selection base memory address for the chromosome population, where chromosomes reside. The second address (address SB) is the population size register, which indicates how many chromosomes are in the population.

Selection is performed iteratively by a loop, which starts at a random location between the base address and the end address, by computing a random offset between 0 and the population size. The following C code followed by its MOVE equivalent illustrates selection.

```
chromosome selection(chromosome c[])
 {
    chromosome select;
    select.gene         = 0L;
    select.fitness      = 0.0f;

        asm Move &c, SELECT_POP_FIRST_REG;
        asm Move POP_SIZE + &c, SELECT_POP_LAST_REG;
        asm Move SELECT_REG, select->gene;

    eval_fitness(&select);

    return select;

 }/* end selection */
```

Another random value is the minimum accumulated fitness, $0.0 \le r \le 1.0$. Once the random starting point and the minimum accumulated fitness are computed, a chromosome is moved into the fitness register. Then the fitness value is added and accumulated.

If the fitness value accumulated is less than the minimum fitness, the selection process continues to the next memory address. The next chromosome is then selected in the same manner. Once two chromosomes have been selected, crossover then occurs. After selecting one chromosome, there is a probability that the one chromosome will be chosen for mutation, in which case it is moved into the mutation register, then into the next generation population.

Another register indicates the base address of where the base population starts, and another register indicates a count of the number of chromosomes in the next generation population, which is initially set to zero.

11.3.1.4 Crossover

Crossover uses two registers, one for each chromosome. When two chromosomes are moved into the registers, the resultant chromosomes are stored in two output registers. Otherwise, each cycle would cause crossover for the offspring if they were put in the original registers. Crossover is commutative, that is, chromosome X and chromosome Y can be transposed, with the same offspring as a result. Crossover is illustrated in the following C code and MOVE OISC equivalent:

```
chromosome selection(chromosome c[])
{
      chromosome select;
        select.gene        = 0L;
        select.fitness     = 0.0f;

        asm Move &c, SELECT_POP_FIRST_REG;
        asm Move POP_SIZE + &c, SELECT_POP_LAST_REG;
        asm Move SELECT_REG, select->gene;

      eval_fitness(&select);

      return select;
}/* end crossover */
```

The crossover mechanism used is ideally uniform. The crossover register will randomly interchange each bit in the parent chromosomes binary bits, and then move the offspring into the next generation population. This is illustrated by the following code:

```
chromosome *crossover(chromosome *x, chromosome *y)
{
      chromosome *offspring = malloc(CHROM_SIZE);
      offspring->gene = 0L;   /* offspring->gene= 0L; */
      offspring->fitness = 0.0;

    /*Move 64-bit long int crossover operandam */
          asm Move x->gene, CROSSOVER_OPA_REG;

    /* Move 64-bit long into crossover operandum */
          asm Move y->gene, CROSSOVER_OPU_REG;
          asm Move OFFSPRING_REG, offspring->gene;

      eval_fitness(offspring);
      return offspring;

}/* end crossover */
```

11.3.1.5 Mutation

If a chromosome is chosen to be mutated, the chromosome is loaded into the mutation register, which randomly inverts bits of the chromosome. Random bit selection has a 0.5 probability of mutating a bit to its current value, in effect, decreasing the probability for mutation on a bit by one half. Once mutation is complete, the chromosome is moved into the next generation population.

As each chromosome is moved into the next generation population, the fitness can be computed and compared to a desired fitness parameter in a memory location. When the algorithm generates a chromosome that meets the minimum fitness, the algorithm can stop, or the chromosome could be moved into the next generation population. The same chromosome could then be sent to an output register, which contains the best possible solution to the problem so far. Mutation can be coded in the following way:

```
chromosome *mutate(chromosome* c)
 {

/*move the gene 64-bit long into the mutation register*/
          asm Move c->gene, MUTATE_REG;

/* move the mutated gene back into the chromosome */
          asm Move MUTATE_REG, c->gene;

    eval_fitness(c);
    return c;
 }/* end mutate */
```

11.3.1.6 Universal Implementation

It should be restated that the select, crossover, and mutation processors could themselves be implemented using MOVE or SBN based OISC. Similarly, the GA OISC architecture could be implemented using SBN elements or both MOVE and SBN, since it has been shown that either element could be implemented using the other.

11.4   Image Processing

The first attempts to use non-systolic OISC processors for imaging applications began in the early 1990s [Laplante91a]. These early attempts were somewhat frustrated by the lack of per-pixel processing power to handle the high computational cost of the algorithms. Fortunately, modern per-pixel processors, transputers, and FPGA architectures offer sufficient compute power to make dedicated OISC image processors a reality.

As a basis for an implementation example consider the case of binary valued images on an image display. It is desired to construct a OISC solution that can perform erosion and dilation of two images – important morphological operations with wide applications [Dougherty88]. This text will focus on image representation in the system, then demonstrate how these functions can be implemented using SBN, HA and MOVE based OISC – all on an underlying FPGA.

11.4.1   Image Representation and Operations

The object space, S, is modeled as a finite subset of the Euclidean space. Once the object's image is captured via an imaging system, the model of underlying space is a finite subset of the Cartesian coordinates. For example, if a 1K × 1K camera is used to capture the image, the image space is assumed be *j* and each (i, j) is called a pixel. The lower left hand corner of the display represents the point $(0,0)$ (see Fig. 11-6).

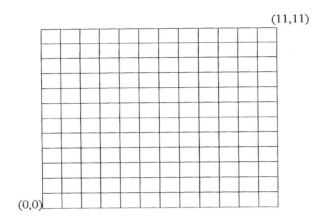

Figure 11-6. A 12 by 12 image display space.

Two basic operations, dilation and erosion, are used to construct filters for images in this setting. The set *B* is the structuring element or probe, where image *B* is the one to be filtered. The erosion operation acts to remove noise and trim edges. The dilation operation is used for filling and smoothing.

A common point wise definition of these operations for sets $A, B \subseteq S$ is

$$\text{DILATE}(A, B)(x, y) = \bigcup_{a \in A} \{a + b \mid b \in B\} \qquad (11\text{-}1)$$

$$\text{ERODE}(A, B)(x, y) = \left[\text{DILATE}(A^c, -B)(x, y) \right]^c \qquad (11\text{-}2)$$

where $+$ is vector addition of the coordinates, A^c represents twos complementation of all the gray values of *A* and $-B$ is simple 180° rotation of image *B* about the origin. Numerous examples of both dilation and erosion can be found throughout the image processing literature [Dougherty88].

Two composite operations, opening and closing can be constructed from the basic erosion and dilation operations. Opening and closing are defined as follows:

$$\text{OPEN}(A, B) = \text{DILATE}\left[\text{ERODE}(A, B), B \right] \qquad (11\text{-}3)$$

$$\text{CLOSE}(A, B) = \text{ERODE}\left[\text{DILATE}(A, -B), -B \right]. \qquad (11\text{-}4)$$

A filter F can be constructed from the composition of opening and closing as follows

$$F(A,B) = \text{CLOSE}\left[\text{OPEN}(A,B), B\right]. \qquad (11\text{-}5)$$

This filtering methodology is known to give quite good restoration results.

In addition to filtering, feature detection can be performed using these basic operations via the hit-or-miss transform $\otimes$. That is, to detect feature B in image A define

$$A \otimes \langle B, B^c \rangle = \text{ERODE}(A,B) \cap \text{ERODE}(A^c, B^c). \qquad (11\text{-}6)$$

The result of this filtration will be the detected image B (if present). Numerous examples of both filtration and feature detection using these techniques can be found throughout the image processing literature [Dougherty88].

Thus the basic operations of dilation, erosion and the more primitive operations of complementation, translation, and rotation are sufficient to perform a large variety of image processing functions. All that must be done is to show how these can be implemented using OISC in FPGAs.

11.4.2   Implementations in OISC

The next sections show how the two basic morphological operations can be implemented using the three basic OISC instructions. The first two sections are less detailed, proof-of-concept treatments, while the subsequent section is a detailed work through of using a MOVE based OISC. The equivalencies of MOVE, SBN, and half adder approaches provide further justification of the first two methodologies.

11.4.2.1 Half Adder Implementation

Fig. 11-7 shows the implementation of the dilation operation using HA CLBs. For image A and structuring element B the key operation is vector addition. This is implemented using the AND and ADD instructions, which have been built entirely using HA elements. Pixel coordinates that exceed the allowable display limits will be clipped if the additive overflow is ignored. Notice how the structure of the circuit is similar to Fig. 11-2(b).

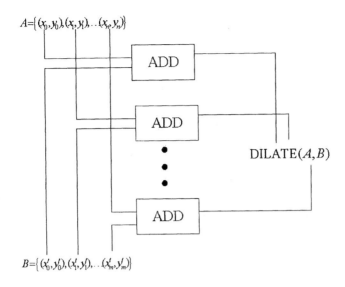

Figure 11-7. Circuit and block diagram for dilation operation.

The solution in Fig. 11-7 requires additional circuitry (not shown) to sequence the selection of point pairs from the image to be filtered and the probe. In essence, this is a nested for-loop, which can be easily implemented [Xu89].

Similarly, the erosion operation can be derived from dilation and set complementation via equation (11-2). Equations (11-3) through (11-6) can be implemented via composition of these operations.

Indeed, while the architectures shown in Fig. 11-7 requires sequential calculation synchronized with a clock, there are parallel implementations as well. For example, one of the most popular computer architectures is the neighborhood connected processors array in which pixels are distributed over the processor elements in a one to one correspondence, and each processor element is connected with its eight nearest neighbors (Fig. 11-8).

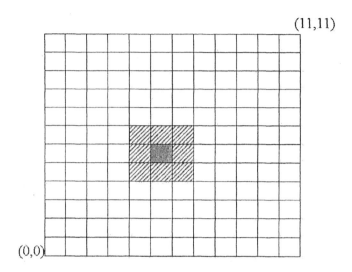

Figure 11-8. Nearest neighbors to pixel at (5,5).

In this arrangement, dilation can be achieved at this point with the eight neighboring pixels in parallel– if the neighbor pixels are contained in the probe [Xu89]. In any other case, additional parallel operations will be needed to complete the dilation of the image with the probe.

Hence, all morphological operations in which the structuring elements used are subsets of the neighborhood set can be implemented in one parallel step [Xu89]. However, it has been further shown that a sequence of neighborhood operations can be used to quickly implement dilation for an arbitrary structuring element, using additional steps [Xu89]. These properties show that parallelization in FPGA-based OISC is straightforward.

11.4.2.2 SBN Implementation

Suppose it is desired to implement the ADD instruction for X and Y, which are memory locations containing the addends. Assume that R1 and R2 are scratch memory locations (or registers) and PC is a memory location containing the program counter – simply another memory location or register. Normally the program counter, auto increments, and the next instruction is executed sequentially. In the cases where the result of an instruction is negative, placing the PC in the branch-address field insures that the next instruction in sequence is executed. The branch field can be changed to be one other than the PC if a true branch is desired. In this way the ADD operation is implemented as follows:

```
SBN R1,R1        ; clear R1
SBN R1,X,PC      ; put -X in R1
SBN R1,Y,PC      ; put -X-Y into R1
SBN R2,R2, PC    ; clear R2
SBN R2,R1, PC    ; R2 contains X + Y
```

The resultant ADD CLB can be replicated to realize the circuit shown in Fig. 11-2 (b). Finally, by cascading the ADD CLB, the circuit in Fig. 11-9 can be realized.

11.4.2.3 MOVE Implementation

Because the MOVE architecture is the most flexible, implementing erosion and dilation presumes that there are processing elements in the memory-mapped space that can perform these operations. In this case, equations (11-1) through (11-6) can be implemented if existing dilate, erode and complement CLBs exist. Fig. 11-9 illustrates the architecture for a MOVE-based imaging processor. In terms of implementation in an FPGA, the HA solution could be the means by which the netlist for the morphological operations is obtained.

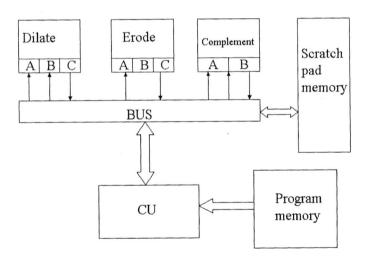

Figure 11-9. Architecture for a MOVE-based OISC Image Processing Machine.

Consider an example. For a 40 by 40 binary image display, A, memory buffer is initialized as all zero (representing a "blank" display). Then for binary image B, which is assumed to have been captured via a camera, and binary probe image C, which has been predetermined based on an appropriate algorithm, the dilation of B by C is given by the code:

```
for(i=0; i<40; i++) {
  for(j=0; j<40; j++) {
    for(k=0; k<40; k++) {
      for(l=0; l<40; l++) {
        A[i+k][j+l]= B[i][j]*C[k][l]);
      }
    }
  }
}
```

Complementation of image A can be handled as follows:

```
for(i=0; i<40; i++) {
  for(j=0; j<40; j++) {
    A[i][j]= A[i] [j] ^ 1);
  }
}
```

And 180° rotation of image A coded as

```
for(i=0; i<40; i++) {
  for(j=0; j<40; j++) {
    A[i][j]= A[j] [i]);
  }
}
```

Composition of these functions as per equations (11-2) through (11-5) yields all of the necessary morphological operations.

Clearly this code can be made more efficient by skipping all zero pixels. In addition, boundary testing is needed to deal with the case of exceeding the display limits in the dilation algorithm. However, the intention here is to make the translation to OISC as straightforward as possible. Boundary violations can be handled easily in hardware.

It remains to be seen how to convert this code to a MOVE-based OISC. This is done for the dilation algorithm only. Conversion of the code for complementation and rotation follow the same methodology.

First the code is hand compiled into a generic 6502 like assembly language. Hand compiling was chosen because it provides better insight into the process. Appendix A shows a line-by-line mixed listing of the C source code and assembly language translation. Some of the more mundane and compiler specific prologue information has been left out for clarity.

The key formula for arrays is of the form

```
A[i1, i2] =  base +((i1 -low1) * n2 + i2 - low2) * w      (11-7)
```

where `low1`, `low2` are the lower bounds, `i1`, `i2` are the indices. `n2` is the number of values `i2` can take. Aho et al [Ah085] gives the recursive recurrence relation. In this case the width w is 1, and the lower bounds are 0. So equation (11-7) simplifies to:

```
A[i1, i2] =   base + (i1 * n2 + i2) * 1            (11-8)
```

in this case n2 = DIM. (DIM was used for a named constant in the for-loops). Hence,

```
A[i1, i2] =  base + (i1 * DIM + i2)               (11-9)
```

Then it is a matter of computing for each array the element for A, B, C. The procedure is similar for the nested for loops, so the code is somewhat a recurring a pattern.

Appendix B shows the only the assembly language equivalent code for the four by four dilation algorithm in its entirety. Appendix C shows the mapping templates for the 6502-like assembly language into the MOVE OISC equivalent code[8]. Ordinarily, an automatic compiler for the actual code would use such a table generation phase. Finally, Appendix D shows the complete OISC equivalent code. This code is ready for mapping into a netlist targeted for a soft MOVE-based OISC, which would have been previously implemented on the FPGA.

11.5   Future Work with OISC

11.5.1   Cellular and Biological Computing

The possibility of building computers based on simple instructions such as the half adder, suggests implementations of such computers in alternate materials or even living organisms. Indeed it has already been suggested that living cells might be used to build a practical computer.

One approach to a living computer is based on the assertion that the interaction between a cell, certain proteins, and DNA can be modeled by the

---

[8] Note that in the C code, two instructions are redundant, NOP and INCrement.

partial finite state automaton shown in Fig. 11-10, and the fact that such an automaton can be used to build half adders [Feitelson02]. Here the central theme is that an input DNA strand is transformed via a series of operations, namely, transcription and translation, into a protein. More specifically, a series of bases off the template DNA are read, and according to the rules of Watson-Crick base pairing, are written as the complementary string on a second DNA in a massively parallel fashion. In one gram of DNA there are on the order of 10^{18} or more DNA strands. In one experiment, each of these strands has been shown to perform the basic operation [Reif02].

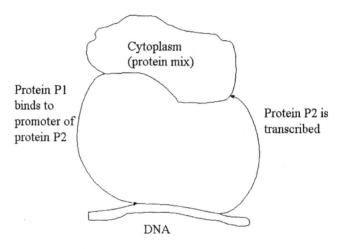

Figure 11-10. A finite state automaton that models the interaction between a cell, certain proteins and DNA [Feitelson02].

The FSA models the interaction between the cell's cytoplasm and DNA strand in which a protein from the cell binds to the promoter of the protein offered by the DNA strand. The cell's cytoplasm and the DNA represent the states for the FSA. The alphabet is the set of proteins encountered by the cell.

The FSA shown in Fig. 11-10 can be generalized by the FSA shown in Fig. 11-11.

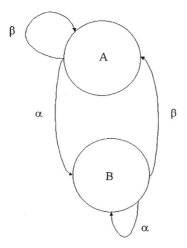

Figure 11-11. A generalized version of the cell FSA shown in Fig. 11-10.

Fig. 11-11 has matrix representation given by Table 11-2

Table 11-2. Transition table for finite state machine given in Fig. 11-13.

	A	B
α	B	A
β	A	B

Encoding α=1, β=0, A=0 and B=1, yields the truth table shown in Table 11-3

Table 11-3. Truth table corresponding to Table 11-2

	0	1
1	1	0
0	0	1

Finally, rewriting the column, row and internal entries as a truth table yields the matrix format finite state machine shown in Table 11-4.

Table 11-4. Finite state machine corresponding to the truth table shown in Table 11-3.

Input	State	Next State
0	0	0
0	1	1
1	0	1
1	1	0

This is simply the truth table for A XOR B. Hence a cell of this type can behave as an XOR gate.

Now if the behavior of the FSA is subject to changes in the proteins, then an alternate representation for Fig. 11-10 is shown in Fig. 11-12 [Feitelson02].

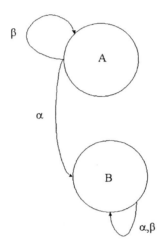

Figure 11-12. An alternate representation for the cell/protein/DNA interaction shown in Fig. 11-10.

Now the matrix representation for the FSA in Fig. 11-12 is shown in Table 11-5.

Table 11-5. Matrix representation of finite state machine given in Fig. 11-15.

	A	B
α	B	B
β	A	B

Encoding α=0, β=1, A=1 and B=0, yields the truth table given in Table 11-6.

Table 11-6. Truth table corresponding to the finite state machine given in Table 11-5.

	1	0
0	0	0
1	1	0

Finally, rewriting the column, row, and internal entries as a truth table, yields the truth table shown in Table 11-7.

Table 11-7. Finite state machine corresponding to truth table given in Table 11-6.

Input	State	Next State
0	0	0
0	0	0
1	0	0
1	1	1

This is simply the truth table for A AND B. Hence a cell of this type appears to behave like an AND gate.

This leads to the conclusion that, depending on the cell/protein/DNA interactions asserted, it appears to be possible to implement a half adder using the AND and XOR cell behaviors.

11.5.2   Implementations of OISC Processor and Compiler

OISC has been examined from a hypothetical and theoretical viewpoint. Another area for further work is to implement a working OISC processor. It should be noted that a number of OISC processor simulators can be found on the Web. These are typically student projects, instructor demos, or proofs of concept.

Once a processor is implemented, further work on optimizing processor operations and functionality can be explored. The overall power of OISC in software has been examined in this book, but not the power in the hardware of a OISC processor. Intuitively, it might seem that OISC being the "ultimate RISC" processor might take the hardware advantages of RISC to an extreme degree. Yet so often what appears intuitively to be true in practice is unfounded or often just wrong. Implementing and exploring the hardware properties of n OISC processor would clarify and resolve such a possibility.

Likewise, having a OISC processor would require a OISC compiler. The compiler technology would have to be different to compile a high-level language such as C or FORTRAN into a one instruction set. The possibility of creating a software model of the underlying OISC architecture for different problem categories is a new direction for compiling. The OISC compiler follows the OISC processor in opening up a new area for exploration that conventional processors do not. Compilers for RISC architectures were initially different and opened up new areas that later became part of the technical field. A OISC processor followed by a OISC compiler for a high-level language would do that. The advent of cross-compilation on OISC processors with different functionality would be another avenue of further work with OISC.

11.5.3   Search for Other OISC Instructions

The key instruction of one instruction set computing discussed in this text has been essentially a MOVE instruction. MOVE -based OISC uses a "naked" MOVE, while subtract and branch if negative is a MOVE but with additional processing. SBN degenerates into its basic sibling instruction for operations that cannot be computed through it. This leaves the one outstanding question, "Is there another instruction that will work with one instruction computing?" It is unclear whether there is a definitive answer to this fundamental question.

Such a "new" OISC instruction would have to be highly orthogonal to synthesize the other more complex instructions required by a processor. MOVE essentially binds basic functionality in a generalized form, and provides a consistent means through the memory space to access the functionality. SBN incorporates additional processing, but at its core is a MOVE.

Orthogonality is not the only requirement; the ability to process the operands to alter the state of the processor is necessary. This property can be termed "operative." Otherwise, the instruction and corresponding processor that uses it is unusable. For example, the hypothetical "GOTO" instruction was a one instruction computer that did nothing to alter the state of the processor, or operands, and hence, was incomplete.

Another line of investigation is the construction of a proof either confirming or denying the possibility of another single instruction. Alternatively, discovering such an instruction and mapping it into the two known variants of OISC. This would be desirable, though this discovery would not rule out the existence of other one instruction computers.

11.6   Exercises

1. In what other areas does the concept of computing with one instruction have applications?

2. In the applications for one instruction computing, what are the shared traits (if any) in the areas in which one instructions can be used? Is there an emerging theme among the applications?

3. Does one instruction set computing have a future as a general-purpose intermediate language for a variety of different platforms? Why or why not?

4. Is there an application for one instruction in future high-level languages? What might some of the features of the newer programming languages be if they emit code for a one instruction computer?

5. Does the one instruction set seem a natural metaphor for alternative models such as biological, optical, quantum, or DNA computing?

6. If there are other kinds of one instruction computers, what would be significant about them in relation to the existing instructions?

7. Is the stored program concept still applicable to computers that are implemented as one instruction machines? If not, what then would be the underlying principle for programmability?

8. What are other singular phenomena of a unified principle? Describe the phenomena and the field where it is found.

9. Does a search for a unified principal look for underlying simplicity (e.g. in physics, a unified field theory), or does it lead to a complexity of one with various combinations?

10. What is the difference between natural phenomena of a unified principle and man-made attempts at singular phenomena?

11. Review your responses to the questions at the end of Chapter 1. Would you still answer these questions the same way?

Appendix A

A GENERIC MICROPROCESSOR AND OISC

For the purpose of illustration a fictitious 1-address microprocessor is described via its instruction set. MOVE equivalent instructions are given then for each instruction. These instructions are referred to throughout the text, and particularly in Chapter 9.

The MOVE OISC consists of the following functional registers

- program_counter
- accumulator
- comparator
- adder
- subtractor
- divider
- ge_target
- gt_target
- lt_target
- eq_target
- ne_target

and the following specialty memory locations are available.

- $run_stack_ptr
- $temp
- $param_stack_ptr

The instructions for the fictitious computer and their MOVE OISC equivalents are given in Table A-1.

Table A-1. A generic computer instruction set and their MOVE OISC equivalents.

Instruction	OISC Equivalent	Description
ADA x	MOVE x, adder	Add to accumulator

ADD x, y	MOVE x, accumulator
	MOVE y, adder
	MOVE accumulator, y
		Add two memory locations

BEQ x	MOVE x, eq_target	Branch equal to
BGE x	MOVE x, ge_target	Branch greater equal to
BGT x	MOVE x, gt_target	Branch greater than
BLT x	MOVE x, lt_target	Branch less than
BNE x	MOVE x, ne_target	Branch not equal to
CMA x	MOVE x, accumulator	Compare memory to accumulator
CMP x,y	MOVE x, accumulator MOVE y, comparator	Compare two memory locations

DEC x	MOVE #1, accumulator
	MOVE x, subtractor
	MOVE accumulator, x
		Decrement memory location

DIV x, y	MOVE x, accumulator
	MOVE y, divider
	MOVE accumulator, y
		Divide two memory locations

INC x	MOVE #1, accumulator
	MOVE x, adder
	MOVE accumulator, x
		Increment memory location

JMP x	MOVE x, program_counter	Jump to x
LDA x	MOVE x, accumulator	Load accumulator
NOP	MOVE $0, $0	No-op

PUSH x	MOVE x, $(param_stack_ptr)
	MOVE #1, accumulator
	MOVE $param_stack_ptr, adder
	MOVE accumulator, param_stack_ptr
		Push onto stack

RET	MOVE $run_stack_ptr, $temp
	MOVE #1, accumulator
	MOVE $run_stack_ptr, subtractor
	MOVE accumulator, $run_stack_ptr
	MOVE $temp, program_counter
		Return from subroutine

STA x	MOVE accumulator, x	Store

Appendix B

ONE INSTRUCTION SET COMPUTER IMPLEMENTATION

This appendix shows how a OISC can make use of existing support software, such as high-level language compilers by mimicking existing processors in this case, the old MOS Technology 6502 processor. This processor was chosen because of its simplicity and its historic importance. Indeed, it can still be found in many older implementations and extensive support software for it is still available on the Web.

First the 6502 opcodes are given. Next, they are simulated using a MOVE-based OISC.

B.1 6502 Opcodes Summary

ADC (ADd with Carry)
Affects Flags: S V Z C

MODE	SYNTAX	HEX	LEN	TIM
Immediate	ADC #$44	$69	2	2
Zero Page	ADC $44	$65	2	3
Zero Page,X	ADC $44,X	$75	2	4
Absolute	ADC $4400	$6D	3	4
Absolute,X	ADC $4400,X	$7D	3	4+
Absolute,Y	ADC $4400,Y	$79	3	4+
Indirect,X	ADC ($44,X)	$61	2	6
Indirect,Y	ADC ($44),Y	$71	2	5+

AND (bitwise AND with accumulator)
Affects Flags: S Z

MODE	SYNTAX	HEX	LEN	TIM
Immediate	AND #$44	$29	2	2
Zero Page	AND $44	$25	2	2
Zero Page,X	AND $44,X	$35	2	3
Absolute	AND $4400	$2D	3	4
Absolute,X	AND $4400,X	$3D	3	4+
Absolute,Y	AND $4400,Y	$39	3	4+
Indirect,X	AND ($44,X)	$21	2	6
Indirect,Y	AND ($44),Y	$31	2	5+

ASL (Arithmetic Shift Left)
Affects Flags: S Z C

MODE	SYNTAX	HEX	LEN	TIM
Accumulator	ASL A	$0A	1	2
Zero Page	ASL $44	$06	2	5
Zero Page,X	ASL $44,X	$16	2	6
Absolute	ASL $4400	$0E	3	6
Absolute,X	ASL $4400,X	$1E	3	7

BIT (test BITs)
Affects Flags: N V Z

MODE	SYNTAX	HEX	LEN	TIM
Zero Page	BIT $44	$24	2	3
Absolute	BIT $4400	$2C	3	4

Branch Instructions
Affect Flags: none

MNEMONIC	HEX
BPL (Branch on PLus)	$10
BMI (Branch on MInus)	$30
BVC (Branch on oVerflow Clear)	$50
BVS (Branch on oVerflow Set)	$70
BCC (Branch on Carry Clear)	$90
BCS (Branch on Carry Set)	$B0
BNE (Branch on Not Equal)	$D0
BEQ (Branch on EQual)	$F0
BRK (BReaK)	

Affects Flags: B

MODE	SYNTAX	HEX	LEN	TIM
Implied	BRK	$00	1	7

CMP (CoMPare accumulator)
Affects Flags: S Z C

MODE	SYNTAX	HEX	LEN	TIM
Immediate	CMP #$44	$C9	2	2
Zero Page	CMP $44	$C5	2	3
Zero Page,X	CMP $44,X	$D5	2	4
Absolute	CMP $4400	$CD	3	4
Absolute,X	CMP $4400,X	$DD	3	4+
Absolute,Y	CMP $4400,Y	$D9	3	4+
Indirect,X	CMP ($44,X)	$C1	2	6
Indirect,Y	CMP ($44),Y	$D1	2	5+ A

CPX (ComPare X register)
Affects Flags: S Z C

MODE	SYNTAX	HEX	LEN	TIM
Immediate	CPX #$44	$E0	2	2
Zero Page	CPX $44	$E4	2	3
Absolute	CPX $4400	$EC	3	4

CPY (ComPare Y register)
Affects Flags: S Z C

MODE	SYNTAX	HEX	LEN	TIM
Immediate	CPY #$44	$C0	2	2
Zero Page	CPY $44	$C4	2	3
Absolute	CPY $4400	$CC	3	4

DEC (DECrement memory)
Affects Flags: S Z

MODE	SYNTAX	HEX	LEN	TIM
Zero Page	DEC $44	$C6	2	5
Zero Page,X	DEC $44,X	$D6	2	6
Absolute	DEC $4400	$CE	3	6
Absolute,X	DEC $4400,X	$DE	3	7

EOR (bitwise Exclusive OR)
Affects Flags: S Z

MODE	SYNTAX	HEX	LEN	TIM
Immediate	EOR #$44	$49	2	2
Zero Page	EOR $44	$45	2	3
Zero Page,X	EOR $44,X	$55	2	4
Absolute	EOR $4400	$4D	3	4
Absolute,X	EOR $4400,X	$5D	3	4+
Absolute,Y	EOR $4400,Y	$59	3	4+
Indirect,X	EOR ($44,X)	$41	2	6
Indirect,Y	EOR ($44),Y	$51	2	5+

Flag (Processor Status) Instructions
Affect Flags: as noted

MNEMONIC	HEX
CLC (CLear Carry)	$18
SEC (SEt Carry)	$38
CLI (CLear Interrupt)	$58
SEI (SEt Interrupt)	$78
CLV (CLear oVerflow)	$B8
CLD (CLear Decimal)	$D8
SED (SEt Decimal)	$F8

INC (INCrement memory)
Affects Flags: S Z

MODE	SYNTAX	HEX	LEN	TIM
Zero Page	INC $44	$E6	2	5
Zero Page,X	INC $44,X	$F6	2	6
Absolute	INC $4400	$EE	3	6
Absolute,X	INC $4400,X	$FE	3	7

JMP (JuMP)
Affects Flags: none

MODE	SYNTAX	HEX	LEN	TIM
Absolute	JMP $5597	$4C	3	3
Indirect	JMP ($5597)	$6C	3	5

JSR (Jump to SubRoutine)
Affects Flags: none

MODE	SYNTAX	HEX	LEN	TIM
Absolute	JSR $5597	$20	3	6

LDA (LoaD Accumulator)
Affects Flags: S Z

MODE	SYNTAX	HEX	LEN	TIM
Immediate	LDA #$44	$A9	2	2
Zero Page	LDA $44	$A5	2	3
Zero Page,X	LDA $44,X	$B5	2	4
Absolute	LDA $4400	$AD	3	4
Absolute,X	LDA $4400,X	$BD	3	4+
Absolute,Y	LDA $4400,Y	$B9	3	4+
Indirect,X	LDA ($44,X)	$A1	2	6
Indirect,Y	LDA ($44),Y	$B1	2	5+

LDX (LoaD X register)
Affects Flags: S Z

MODE	SYNTAX	HEX	LEN	TIM
Immediate	LDX #$44	$A2	2	2
Zero Page	LDX $44	$A6	2	3
Zero Page,Y	LDX $44,Y	$B6	2	4
Absolute	LDX $4400	$AE	3	4
Absolute,Y	LDX $4400,Y	$BE	3	4+

LDY (LoaD Y register)
Affects Flags: S Z

MODE	SYNTAX	HEX	LEN	TIM
Immediate	LDY #$44	$A0	2	2
Zero Page	LDY $44	$A4	2	3
Zero Page,X	LDY $44,X	$B4	2	4
Absolute	LDY $4400	$AC	3	4
Absolute,X	LDY $4400,X	$BC	3	4+

LSR (Logical Shift Right)
Affects Flags: S Z C

MODE	SYNTAX	HEX	LEN	TIM
Accumulator	LSR A	$4A	1	2
Zero Page	LSR $44	$46	2	5
Zero Page,X	LSR $44,X	$56	2	6
Absolute	LSR $4400	$4E	3	6
Absolute,X	LSR $4400,X	$5E	3	7

NOP (No OPeration)
Affects Flags: none

MODE	SYNTAX	HEX	LEN	TIM
Implied	NOP	$EA	1	2

ORA (bitwise OR with Accumulator)
Affects Flags: S Z

MODE	SYNTAX	HEX	LEN	TIM
Immediate	ORA #$44	$09	2	2
Zero Page	ORA $44	$05	2	2
Zero Page,X	ORA $44,X	$15	2	3
Absolute	ORA $4400	$0D	3	4
Absolute,X	ORA $4400,X	$1D	3	4+
Absolute,Y	ORA $4400,Y	$19	3	4+
Indirect,X	ORA ($44,X)	$01	2	6
Indirect,Y	ORA ($44),Y	$11	2	5+

Register Instructions
Affect Flags: S Z

MNEMONIC	HEX
TAX (Transfer A to X)	$AA
TXA (Transfer X to A)	$8A
DEX (DEcrement X)	$CA
INX (INcrement X)	$E8
TAY (Transfer A to Y)	$A8
TYA (Transfer Y to A)	$98
DEY (DEcrement Y)	$88
INY (INcrement Y)	$C8

ROL (ROtate Left)
Affects Flags: S Z C

ODE	SYNTAX	HEX	LEN	TIM
Accumulator	ROL A	$2A	1	2
Zero Page	ROL $44	$26	2	5
Zero Page,X	ROL $44,X	$36	2	6
Absolute	ROL $4400	$2E	3	6
Absolute,X	ROL $4400,X	$3E	3	7

ROR (ROtate Right)
Affects Flags: S Z C

MODE	SYNTAX	HEX	LEN	TIM
Accumulator	ROR A	$6A	1	2
Zero Page	ROR $44	$66	2	5
Zero Page,X	ROR $44,X	$76	2	6
Absolute	ROR $4400	$6E	3	6
Absolute,X	ROR $4400,X	$7E	3	7

RTI (ReTurn from Interrupt)
Affects Flags: all

MODE	SYNTAX	HEX	LEN	TIM
Implied	RTI	$40	1	6

RTS (ReTurn from Subroutine)
Affects Flags: none

MODE	SYNTAX	HEX	LEN	TIM
Implied	RTS	$60	1	6

SBC (SuBtract with Carry)
Affects Flags: S V Z C

MODE	SYNTAX	HEX	LEN	TIM
Immediate	SBC #$44	$E9	2	2
Zero Page	SBC $44	$E5	2	3
Zero Page,X	SBC $44,X	$F5	2	4
Absolute	SBC $4400	$ED	3	4
Absolute,X	SBC $4400,X	$FD	3	4+
Absolute,Y	SBC $4400,Y	$F9	3	4+
Indirect,X	SBC ($44,X)	$E1	2	6
Indirect,Y	SBC ($44),Y	$F1	2	5+

STA (STore Accumulator)
Affects Flags: none

MODE	SYNTAX	HEX	LEN	TIM
Zero Page	STA $44	$85	2	3
Zero Page,X	STA $44,X	$95	2	4
Absolute	STA $4400	$8D	3	4
Absolute,X	STA $4400,X	$9D	3	5
Absolute,Y	STA $4400,Y	$99	3	5
Indirect,X	STA ($44,X)	$81	2	6
Indirect,Y	STA ($44),Y	$91	2	6

Stack Instructions

MNEMONIC	HEX	TIM
TXS (Transfer X to Stack ptr)	$9A	2
TSX (Transfer Stack ptr to X)	$BA	2
PHA (PusH Accumulator)	$48	3
PLA (PuLl Accumulator)	$68	4
PHP (PusH Processor status)	$08	3
PLP (PuLl Processor status)	$28	4
STX (STore X register)		

Affects Flags: none

MODE	SYNTAX	HEX	LEN	TIM
Zero Page	STX $44	$86	2	3
Zero Page,Y	STX $44,Y	$96	2	4
Absolute	STX $4400	$8E	3	4

STY (STore Y register)
Affects Flags: none

MODE	SYNTAX	HEX	LEN	TIM
Zero Page	STY $44	$84	2	3
Zero Page,X	STY $44,X	$94	2	4
Absolute	STY $4400	$8C	3	4

B.2 6502 Opcodes Mapped to MOVE OISC

ADC (ADd with Carry)

```
MOVE processor_status, accumulator    ;get status register
MOVE BIT_WORD_CARRY,  logical-AND     ;get only carry flag
MOVE accumulator, temp_register       ;store temp result
MOVE user_accumulator, accumulator    ;move user_accumulator to
                                       accumulator
MOVE temp, adder                      ;add carry to user_accumulator
MOVE operand,  adder                  ;add operand to accumulator
MOVE accumulator, user_accumulator    ;store accumulator to users
```

AND (bitwise AND with accumulator)

```
MOVE user_accumulator, accumulator    ;store users accumulator
                                       in actual
MOVE operand, logical-and             ;logical AND with
                                       accumulator
MOVE accumulator, operand             ;store operand
```

ASL (Arithmetic Shift Left)

```
MOVE operand, left-shifter   ; left shift operand
```

BIT (test BITs)

```
;test bit-7
  MOVE operand, accumulator
  MOVE BIT_7_MASK_1, logical-AND
;if result = BIT_7_MASK_1, bit = 1
  MOVE TRUE_7, branch-equal-target
  MOVE BIT_7_MASK_1, comparator

;bit = 0, set negative bit = 0
  MOVE processor_status, accumulator
  MOVE BIT_MASK_NEG_0, logical-AND
  MOVE accumulator, processor_status
  MOVE CONT1, program_counter

;bit = 1, set negative bit = 1
```

```
TRUE7:   MOVE processor_status, accumulator
         MOVE BIT_MASK_NEG_1, logical-OR
         MOVE accumulator, processor_status
   ;test bit-6
CONT1:   MOVE operand, accumulator
         MOVE BIT_6_MASK_1, logical-AND
   ;if result = BIT_6_MASK_1, bit = 1
         MOVE TRUE_6, branch-equal-target
         MOVE BIT_6_MASK_1, comparator

   ;bit = 0, set overflow bit = 0
TRUE6:   MOVE processor_status, accumulator
         MOVE BIT_MASK_OVERFLOW_0, logical-AND
         MOVE accumulator, processor_status
         MOVE CONT2, program_counter
   ;bit = 1, set overflow bit = 1
         MOVE processor_status, accumulator
         MOVE BIT_MASK_OVERFLOW_1, logical-OR
         MOVE accumulator, processor_status
CONT2:
   ;logical AND
         MOVE user-accumulator, accumulator
         MOVE TRUE_0, branch-equal-target
         MOVE operand, logical-AND
         MOVE END_BIT, program_counter

   ;if accumulator = zero, zero-flag set (automatically)
TRUE_0:  MOVE processor_status, accumulator
         MOVE BIT_MASK_ZERO_1, logical-OR
         MOVE accumulator, processor_status
   ;NOP
ENDBIT:  MOVE accumulator, accumulator
```

BPL (Branch on PLus)

```
MOVE branch_address, branch-equal register
MOVE BIT_WORD_PLUS, accumulator
MOVE status register, comparator
BMI (Branch on MInus)

MOVE branch_address, branch-equal register
MOVE BIT_WORD_MINUS, accumulator
MOVE status register, comparator
```

BVC (Branch on oVerflow Clear)

```
MOVE branch_address, branch-equal register
MOVE BIT_WORD_OVERFLOW_CLEAR, accumulator
MOVE status register, comparator
```

BVS (Branch on oVerflow Set)

```
MOVE branch_address, branch-equal register
MOVE BIT_WORD_OVERFLOW_SET, accumulator
MOVE status register, comparator
```

BCC (Branch on Carry Clear)

```
MOVE branch_address, branch-equal register
MOVE BIT_WORD_CARRY_CLEAR, accumulator
MOVE status register, comparator
```

BCS (Branch on Carry Set)

```
MOVE branch_address, branch-equal register
MOVE BIT_CARRY_SET, accumulator
MOVE status register, comparator
```

BNE (Branch on Not Equal)

```
MOVE branch_address, branch-equal register
MOVE BIT_WORD_NOT_EQUAL, accumulator
MOVE status register, comparator
```

BEQ (Branch on EQual)

```
MOVE operand, branch-equal register
MOVE BIT_WORD_EQUAL, accumulator
MOVE status register, comparator
```

BRK (BReaK)

```
;set break bit
MOVE processor_status, accumulator
MOVE BIT_MASK_BREAK_1, logical-OR
MOVE accumulator, processor_status
```

```
;increment program counter push on stack
MOVE program_counter, accumulator
MOVE CONSTANT_ONE, adder
MOVE accumulator, (stack_ptr)

;increment stack pointer
MOVE stack_ptr, accumulator
MOVE CONSTANT_ONE, adder

MOVE accumulator, stack_ptr

;jump to interrupt vector
MOVE interrupt_vector, program_counter
```

CMP (CoMPare accumulator)

```
MOVE user_accumulator, accumulator
MOVE operand, comparator
```

CPX (ComPare X register)

```
MOVE xRegister, accumulator
MOVE operand, comparator
```

CPY (ComPare Y register)

```
MOVE yRegister, accumulator
MOVE operand, comparator
```

DEC (DECrement memory)

```
MOVE operand, accumulator
MOVE CONSTANT_ONE, subtractor
MOVE accumulator, operand
```

EOR (bitwise Exclusive OR)

```
MOVE user_accumulator, accumulator
MOVE operand, logical-XOR
MOVE accumulator, user_accumulator
```

CLC (CLear Carry)

```
MOVE processor_status, accumulator
MOVE BIT_MASK_CARRY_0, logical-AND
MOVE accumulator, processor_status
```

SEC (SEt Carry)

```
MOVE processor_status, accumulator
MOVE BIT_MASK_CARRY_1, logical-OR
MOVE accumulator, processor_status
```

CLI (CLear Interrupt)

```
MOVE processor_status, accumulator
MOVE BIT_MASK_INTERRUPT_0, logical-AND
MOVE accumulator, processor_status
```

SEI (SEt Interrupt)

```
MOVE processor_status, accumulator
MOVE BIT_MASK_INTERRUPT_1, logical-OR
MOVE accumulator, processor_status
```

CLV (CLear oVerflow)

```
MOVE processor_status, accumulator
MOVE BIT_MASK_OVERFLOW_0, logical-AND
MOVE accumulator, processor_status
```

CLD (CLear Decimal)

```
MOVE processor_status, accumulator
MOVE BIT_MASK_DECIMAL_0, logical-AND
MOVE accumulator, processor_status
```

SED (SEt Decimal)

```
MOVE processor_status, accumulator
MOVE BIT_MASK_DECIMAL_1, logical-OR
MOVE accumulator, processor_status
```

INC (INCrement memory)

```
MOVE operand, accumulator
MOVE CONSTANT_ONE, subtractor
MOVE accumulator, operand
```

JMP (JuMP)

MOVE operand, program_counter

JSR (Jump to Subroutine)

MOVE program_counter, (stack_ptr)

MOVE stack_ptr, accumulator
MOVE CONSTANT_ONE, adder
MOVE accumulator, stack_ptr

MOVE operand, program_counter

LDA (LoaD Accumulator)

MOVE operand, user_accumulator

LDX (LoaD X register)

MOVE operand, xRegister

LDY (LoaD Y register)

MOVE operand, yRegister

LSR (Logical Shift Right)

MOVE operand, right-shifter   ; left shift operand
MOVE right-shifter, operand   ; store operand

NOP (No OPeration)

MOVE accumulator, accumulator

ORA (bitwise OR with Accumulator)

MOVE user_accumulator, accumulator
MOVE operand, logical-IOR
MOVE accumulator, user_accumulator

TAX (Transfer A to X)

MOVE user_accumulator, xRegister

TXA (Transfer X to A)

```
MOVE xRegister, user_accumulator
```

DEX (DEcrement X)

```
MOVE xRegister, accumulator
MOVE CONSTANT_ONE, subtractor
MOVE accumulator, xRegister
```

INX (INcrement X)

```
MOVE xRegister, accumulator
MOVE CONSTANT_ONE, adder
MOVE accumulator, xRegister
```

TAY (Transfer A to Y)

```
MOVE user_accumulator, yRegister
```

TYA (Transfer Y to A)

```
MOVE yRegister, user_accumulator
```

DEY (DEcrement Y)

```
MOVE yRegister, accumulator
MOVE CONSTANT_ONE, subtractor
MOVE accumulator, yRegister
```

INY (INcrement Y)

```
MOVE yRegister, accumulator
MOVE CONSTANT_ONE, adder
MOVE accumulator, yRegister
```

ROL (ROtate Left)

```
MOVE user_accumulator, left-rotate register
MOVE left-rotate_register, user_accumulator
```

ROR (ROtate Right)

```
MOVE user_accumulator, right-rotate register
MOVE right-rotate_register, user_accumulator
```

RTI (ReTurn from Interrupt)

```
;PLP
MOVE stack_ptr, accumulator
MOVE CONSTANT_ONE, subtractor
MOVE accumulator, stack_ptr
MOVE (stack_ptr), processor_status

;CLI
MOVE processor_status, accumulator
MOVE BIT_MASK_INTERRUPT_0, logical-AND
MOVE accumulator, processor_status

;RTS
MOVE stack_ptr, accumulator
MOVE CONSTANT_ONE, subtractor
MOVE accumulator, stack_ptr
MOVE (stack_ptr), program_counter
```

RTS (ReTurn from Subroutine)

```
MOVE stack_ptr, accumulator
MOVE CONSTANT_ONE, subtractor
MOVE accumulator, stack_ptr
MOVE (stack_ptr), program_counter
```

SBC (SuBtract with Carry)

```
MOVE processor_status, accumulator     ;get status register
MOVE BIT_WORD_CARRY,  logical-AND      ;get only carry flag
MOVE accumulator, temp_register        ;store temp result
MOVE user_accumulator, accumulator     ;move user_accumulator to
                                       accumulator

MOVE temp, subtractor                  ;subtract carry to
                                       user_accumulator
MOVE operand,  subtractor              ;subtract operand to
                                       accumulator
MOVE accumulator, user_accumulator     ;store accumulator to
                                       users
```

STA (STore Accumulator)

MOVE user_accumulator, operand

TXS (Transfer X to Stack ptr)

MOVE xRegister, stack_ptr

TSX (Transfer Stack ptr to X)

MOVE stack_ptr, xRegister

PHA (PusH Accumulator)

MOVE user_accumulator, (stack_ptr)
MOVE stack_ptr, accumulator
MOVE CONSTANT_ONE, adder
MOVE accumulator, stack_ptr

PLA (PuLl Accumulator)

MOVE stack_ptr, accumulator
MOVE CONSTANT_ONE, subtractor
MOVE accumulator, stack_ptr
MOVE (stack_ptr), user_accumulator

PHP (PusH Processor status)

MOVE processor_status, (stack_ptr)
MOVE stack_ptr, accumulator
MOVE CONSTANT_ONE, adder
MOVE accumulator, stack_ptr

PLP (PuLl Processor status)

MOVE stack_ptr, accumulator
MOVE CONSTANT_ONE, subtractor
MOVE accumulator, stack_ptr
MOVE (stack_ptr), processor_status

STX (STore X register)

MOVE xRegister, operand

STY (STore Y register)

MOVE yRegister, operand

interrupt

```
;set interrupt bit SEI
MOVE processor_status, accumulator
MOVE BIT_MASK_INTERRUPT_1, logical-OR
MOVE accumulator, processor_status

;push program counter on stack
MOVE program_counter, (stack_ptr)

;increment stack pointer
MOVE stack_ptr, accumulator
MOVE CONSTANT_ONE, adder
MOVE accumulator, stack_ptr

;push processor status
MOVE processor_status, (stack_ptr)

MOVE stack_ptr, accumulator
MOVE CONSTANT_ONE, adder
MOVE accumulator, stack_ptr

;jump to interrupt vector
MOVE interrupt_vector, program_counter
```

non-maskable interrupt

```
;set interrupt bit SEI
MOVE processor_status, accumulator
MOVE BIT_MASK_INTERRUPT_1, logical-OR
MOVE accumulator, processor_status

;push program counter on stack
MOVE program_counter, (stack_ptr)

;increment stack pointer
MOVE stack_ptr, accumulator
MOVE CONSTANT_ONE, adder
MOVE accumulator, stack_ptr
```

```
;push processor status
MOVE processor_status, (stack_ptr)

MOVE stack_ptr, accumulator
MOVE CONSTANT_ONE, adder
MOVE accumulator, stack_ptr

;jump to interrupt vector
MOVE nmi_interrupt_vector, program_counter
```

init

```
MOVE INIT_STATUS, processor_status
MOVE init_vector, program_counter
```

B.3 6502 Addressing as MOVE-based OISC

Constant:

Immediate

```
MOVE #operandam, $operandum
```

Variable:

Accumulator (use move processor accumulator)

```
MOVE operandam, $accumulator
```

Implied

```
MOVE operandam, $implied-register
```

Absolute

```
MOVE operandam, $operandum
```

Relative

```
MOVE program_counter, adder
MOVE #operand, accumulator
MOVE accumulator, program_counter
```

Zero Page (operandam on zero-page)

```
MOVE $operandam, $operandum
```

Zero Page X (add register X to operand)

```
MOVE $operandam, adder
MOVE $x_register, accumulator
MOVE accumulator, $operandum
```

Zero Page Y (add register X to operand)

```
MOVE $operandam, adder
MOVE $x_register, accumulator
MOVE accumulator, $operandum
```

Pointer:

Absolute X

```
MOVE $operandam, adder
MOVE $x_register, accumulator
MOVE accumulator, $operandam
MOVE ($operandam), $operandum
```

Absolute Y

```
MOVE $operandam, adder
MOVE $y_register, accumulator
MOVE accumulator, $operandam
MOVE ($operandam), $operandum
```

Indirect

```
MOVE $(operandam), $operandum
```

Indirect X (same as Absolute X only on zero-page)

```
MOVE $operandam, adder
MOVE $x_register, accumulator
MOVE accumulator, $operandam
MOVE ($operandam), $operandum
```

Indirect Y (same as Absolute Y only on zero-page)

```
MOVE $operandam, adder
MOVE $y_register, accumulator
MOVE accumulator, $operandam
MOVE ($operandam), $operandum
```

Registers become memory locations

```
accumulator => $user_accumulator
x_register  => $xRegister
y_register  => $yRegister
```

B.4 6502 Addressing Modes and MOVE-based OISC

Immediate	ADC #03	data immediate normal access
Accumulator	ASL	accumulator memory location, so like absolute
Implied	INX	implicit register memory location, so like absolute
Absolute	JMP $3000	normal memory access
Zero Page	LDA $30	faster access on zero-page, all memory the same
Indirect	JMP ($3300)	normal indirect memory access
Relative	BCC $30	add/subtract before instruction to program counter
Zero Page X	EOR $1000,X	add/subtract zero-page address value with register x
Zero Page Y	XOR $1001,Y	add/subtract zero-page address value with register y
Absolute X	LDA $2000,X	add register X and load from relative memory location
Absolute Y	STA $2001,Y	add register Y and load from relative memory location
Indirect X	STA($30), X	add register X to memory location and load from location
Indirect Y	ORA($20), Y	add register Y to memory location and load from location

Appendix C

DILATION CODE IMPLEMENTATION

This appendix contains source code for the dilation operation and hand compiled mixed listing output showing C instruction and corresponding generic (6502) assembly language translation.

```
#define DIM 40

for(i=0; i<40; i++) {
   for(j=0; j<40; j++) {
      for(k=0; k<40; k++) {
         for(l=0; l<40; l++) {
            A[i+k][j+l]= B[i][j]*C[k][l];
         }
      }
   }
}
```

```
variables: i,j,k,l => address of each variable
Arrays, A, B, C    => base address of each
DIM 40             => memory address of constant

B[i][j]=base + ((i - low_i) * n2 + j - low_j) * w

base + (i * n2 + j) * 1
base + (i * n2) + j
Array [i][j] = base + (i * DIM) + j
```

```
for(i=0; i<DIM; i++)
{
}

i=0;
START: nop
if i > DIM
  goto END

nop

i++
goto START
END: nop
```

```
i=0;                        STO #0, &i; store constant
START_i: nop                NOP;
if i > DIM                  CMP &i, &DIM; compare
  goto END_i;               BGT END_i;

                            NOP; loop body

i++;                        INC &i;
goto START_i;               JMP START_i;
END_i:  nop                 NOP;
```

```
;define DIM as a magic constant  use EQU   DIM EQU #40
STO #40, &DIM

;for loop i
        STO #0, &I    ; store constant
START_i: NOP;
        CMP &i, &DIM ; compare
        BGT END_i;

;for loop j
        STO #0, &j    ; store constant
START_j: NOP;
        CMP &j, &DIM ; compare
        BGT END_i;

;for loop k
        STO #0, &k    ; store constant
START_k: NOP;
        CMP &k, &DIM ; compare
        BGT END_i;

;for loop l
        STO #0, &l    ; store constant
START_l: NOP;
        CMP &l, &DIM ; compare
        BGT END_i;

; code for array access
```

```
; array B access: base B + (i *n2) + j B[i][j]*C[k][l]

        LDO #1,  &tempB     ; init temp to 1
        MUL i,    &tempB    ; temp = temp * i
        MUL DIM, &tempB     ; temp = temp * DIM
        ADD j ,  &tempB     ; temp = temp + j
        ADD &A[0], &tempB   ; temp  =  temp  +  base  A[0]
                              address

; array C access: base B + (k *n2) + l B[i][j]

        LDO #1,  &tempC     ;  init temp to 1
        MUL k,   &tempC     ;  temp = temp * i
        MUL DIM, &tempC     ;  temp = temp * DIM
        ADD l ,  &tempC     ;  temp = temp + j
        ADD &A[0], &tempC   ; temp = temp + base A[0]
                              address

  ; create temporary variables x, y

        LDO #0, &x;
        LDO #0, &y;

        ADD i, &x;
        ADD k, &x;

        ADD j, &y;
        ADD k, &y;

  ; access array A with temporary variables  A[i+k][j+l]

        LDO #1, &tempA      ; init temp to 1
        MUL y,  &tempA      ; temp = temp * i
        MUL DIM,&tempA      ; temp = temp * n2
        ADD x , &tempA      ; temp = temp + j
        ADD &A[0],&tempA    ; temp = temp + base A[0]
                              address
```

```
; do operation on accessed array elements: A[i+k][j+l]=
B[i][j]*C[k][l]
; multiply value at tempB by tempC or tempB = tempB *
tempC
        MUL tempB, tempC
        STO tempB, &tempA      ; store value in tempA

        INC &i;
        JMP START_li;
END_l:  NOP;

        INC &k;
        JMP START_k;
END_k:  NOP;


        INC &j;
        JMP START_i;
END_j:  NOP;

        INC &i;
        JMP START_i;
END_i:  NOP;


base + (i * n2) + j
A[i+k][j+l]= B[i][j]*C[k][l];

; array B access: base B + (i *n2) + j

        LDO #1, &tempB      ; init temp to 1
        MUL i,  &tempB      ; temp = temp * i
        MUL DIM, &tempB     ; temp = temp * DIM
        ADD j , &tempB      ; temp = temp + j
        ADD &A[0], &tempB   ; temp = temp + base A[0]
                             address

; array C access: base B + (k *n2) + l

        LDO #1, &tempC      ; init temp to 1
        MUL k,  &tempC      ; temp = temp * i
        MUL DIM, &tempC     ; temp = temp * DIM
        ADD l , &tempC      ; temp = temp + j
        ADD &A[0], &tempC   ; temp = temp + base A[0]
                             address
; create temporary variables x, y

        LDO #0, &x;
        LDO #0, &y;
        ADD i, &x;
        ADD k, &x;
        ADD j, &y;
        ADD k, &y;
```

```
; access array A with temporary variables

        LDO #1,    &tempA     ; init temp to 1
        MUL y,     &tempA     ; temp = temp * i
        MUL DIM,   &tempA     ; temp = temp * n2
        ADD x ,    &tempA     ; temp = temp + j
        ADD &A[0], &tempA     ; temp = temp + base A[0]
                                address
```

Appendix D

COMPILER OUTPUT FOR DILATION

This appendix contains the compiler output – generic 6502 assembly code for dilation code with corresponding translation to MOVE OISC.

```
;define DIM as a magic constant

DIM        .EQU     40

; directive to originate the program starting address
           '.ORG      $0xCAFEBABE


; for loop i
           STO #0, &i  ; store constant

START_i: NOP;
           CMP &i, DIM  ; compare
           BGT END_i;

; for loop j
           STO #0, &j   ; store constant

START_j: NOP;
           CMP &j, DIM  ; compare
           BGT END_i;

;for loop k
           STO #0, &k   ; store constant

START_k: NOP;
           CMP &k, DIM  ; compare
           BGT END_I    ;

; for loop l
           STO #0, &l   ; store constant
```

```
START_l:  NOP;
          CMP &l, &DIM; compare
          BGT END_I    ;

; code for array access
;array B access: base B + (i *n2) + j B[i][j]*C[k][l]

          STO #1,  &tempB   ; init temp to 1
          MUL i,   &tempB   ; temp = temp * i
          MUL DIM, &tempB   ; temp = temp * DIM
; temp = temp + base A[0] address
          ADD j ,  &tempB   ; temp = temp + j
          ADD &A[0],&tempB
; array C access: base B + (k *n2) + l B[i][j]
          STO #1,  &tempC   ; init temp to 1
          MUL k,   &tempC   ; temp = temp * i
          MUL DIM, &tempC   ; temp = temp * DIM
          ADD l ,  &tempC   ; temp = temp + j
          ADD &A[0],&tempC  ;temp=temp+base address

; create temporary variables x, y

          STO #0, &x;
          STO #0, &y;
          ADD i, &x;
          ADD k, &x;
          ADD j, &y;
          ADD k, &y;

; access array A with temporary variables A[i+k][j+l]

          STO #1,  &tempA    ; init temp to 1
          MUL y,   &tempA    ; temp = temp * i
          MUL DIM, &tempA    ; temp = temp * n2
          ADD x ,  &tempA    ; temp = temp + j
          ADD &A[0],&tempA   ; temp=temp+base address

; do operation on accessed array elements:
A[i+k][j+l]= B[i][j]*C[k][l]

; multiply value at tempB by tempC or tempB = tempB *
tempC
          MUL tempB, tempC
          STO tempB, &tempA  ; store value in tempA
          INC &I
          JMP START_li
```

```
END_l:    NOP;

          INC &k;
          JMP START_k;
END_k:    NOP;

          INC &j;
          JMP START_i;
END_j:    NOP;

          INC &i;
          JMP START_i;
END_i:    NOP;

; directive for end assembly code
          .END
```

Appendix E

OISC EQUIVALENT OF DILATION

This appendix contains the OISC code output from hand compilation of dilation algorithm shown in Appendix C and D and applying the table translation in Appendix B to MOVE code.

```
; for loop i
        MOVE #0, &i; store constant

START_i: MOVE ACC, ACC;
        MOVE &END_i, BGT;
        MOVE &i, ACC;
        MOVE DIM, CMP

; for loop j
        MOVE #0, &j; store constant

START_j: MOVE ACC, ACC;
        MOVE &END_j, BGT;
        MOVE &i, ACC;
        MOVE DIM, CMP

;for loop k
        MOVE #0, &k; store constant

START_k: MOVE ACC, ACC;
        MOVE &END_k, BGT;
        MOVE &i, ACC;
        MOVE DIM, CMP
```

```
; for loop 1
        MOVE #0, &1; store constant

START_1: MOVE ACC, ACC;
         MOVE &END_1, BGT;
         MOVE &i, ACC;
         MOVE DIM, CMP

; code for array access
; array B access: base B + (i *n2) + j
B[i][j]*C[k][l]

        MOVE #1, &tempB ; init temp to 1
        MOVE i, ACC
        MOVE &tempB, MULTI
        MOVE ACC, &tempB

        MOVE DIM, ACC
        MOVE &tempB, MULTI
        MOVE ACC, &tempB

        MOVE j, ACC
        MOVE &tempB, ADDER
        MOVE ACC, &tempB

        MOVE &A[0], ACC
        MOVE &tempB, ADDER
        MOVE ACC, &tempB

; array C access: base B + (k *n2) + l B[i][j]

        MOVE #1, &tempC    ; init temp to 1

        MOVE k, ACC
        MOVE &tempC, MULTI
        MOVE ACC, &tempC

        MOVE DIM, ACC
        MOVE &tempC, MULTI
        MOVE ACC, &tempC

        MOVE l, ACC
        MOVE &tempC, ADDER
        MOVE ACC, &tempC
```

```
        MOVE &A[0], ACC
        MOVE &tempC, ADDER
        MOVE ACC, &tempC

  ; create temporary variables x, y

        MOVE #0, &x;
        MOVE #0, &y;

        MOVE i, ACC
        MOVE &x, ADDER
        MOVE ADDER, &x

        MOVE k, ACC
        MOVE &x, ADDER
        MOVE ACC, &x

        MOVE j, ACC
        MOVE &y, ADDER
        MOVE ACC, &y

        MOVE k, ACC
        MOVE &y, ADDER
        MOVE ACC, &y

  ;   access   array   A   with   temporary   variables
A[i+k][j+l]

        MOVE #1, &tempA     ; init temp to 1

        MOVE y, ACC
        MOVE &tempA, MULTI
        MOVE ACC, &tempA

        MOVE DIM, ACC
        MOVE &tempA, MULTI
        MOVE ACC, &tempA

        MOVE x, ACC
        MOVE &tempA, ADDER
        MOVE ACC, &tempA

        MOVE &A[0], ACC
        MOVE &tempA, ADDER
        MOVE ACC, &tempA
```

```
          ;  do   operation   on   accessed   array   elements:
A[i+k][j+l]= B[i][j]*C[k][l]

              MOVE tempC, ACC
              MOVE tempB, MULTI
              MOVE ACC, tempC

              MOVE tempB, &tempA    ; store value in tempA

              MOVE #1, ACC
              MOVE &i, ADDER
              MOVE ADDER, &l

              MOVE START_l, PC;
  END_l:      MOVE ACC, ACC;

              MOVE #1, ACC
              MOVE &k, ADDER
              MOVE ACC, &k

              MOVE START_k, PC;
  END_k:      MOVE ACC, ACC;

              MOVE #1, ACC
              MOVE &j, ADDER
              MOVE ACC, &j

              MOVE START_i, PC;
  END_j:      MOVE ACC, ACC;

              MOVE #1, ACC
              MOVE &i, ADDER
              MOVE ACC, &l

              MOVE START_i, PC;
  END_i:      MOVE ACC, ACC;
```

GLOSSARY
Selected Basic Terms

Words ought to be a little wild for they are the assaults of thought on the unthinking.

John Maynard Keynes (1883 - 1946), British economist, pioneer of the theory of full employment, and with other interests from book collecting to probability theory.

accumulator – an anonymous register used in certain computer instructions.

activity packet – a special token passed between the processors in a dataflow architecture. Each token contains an opcode, operand count, operands, and a list of destination addresses for the result of the computation.

address bus – the collection of wires needed to access individual memory addresses.

ALU – see arithmetic logic unit.

arithmetic logic unit (ALU) – the CPU internal device that performs arithmetic and logical operations.

assembler – software that translates assembly language to machine code.

assembly language – the set of symbolic equivalents to the macroinstruction set.

associative memory – memory organized so that it can be searched according to its contents.

atomic instruction – an instruction that cannot be interrupted.

bus arbitration – the process of ensuring that only one device at a time can place data on the bus.

bus contention – a condition in which two or more devices attempt to gain control of the main memory bus simultaneously.

bus cycle – memory fetch.

bus grant – a signal provided by the DMA controller to a device indicating that is has exclusive rights to the bus.

bus time-out – a condition whereby a device making a DMA request does not receive a bus grant before some specified time.

cellular automata – a computational paradigm for an efficient description of SIMD massively parallel systems.

CISC – see complex instruction set computer.

compiler – software that translates high-order language programs into assembly code.

complete – an instruction set that is equivalent to a single tape Turing machine.

complex instruction set computer (CISC) – architecture characterized by a large, microcoded instruction set with numerous addressing modes.

condition code register – internal CPU register used to implement a conditional transfer.

conditional branch – a change of the program counter based on the result of a previous test.

content-addressable memory – see associative memory.

control unit (CU) – a complex circuit that orchestrates internal data movement and microinstruction sequencing.

coprocessor – a second specialized CPU used to extend the macroinstruction set.

CPU – central processing unit.

CU – see control unit.

cycle stealing – a situation in which DMA access precludes the CPU from accessing the bus.

data bus – bus used to carry data between the various components in the system.

dataflow architecture – a multiprocessing system that uses a large number of special processors. Computation is performed by passing activity packs between them.

decode – the process of isolating the opcode field of a macroinstruction and determining the address in micromemory of the programming corresponding to it.

direct memory access (DMA) – a scheme in which access to the computer's memory is afforded to other devices in the system without the intervention of the CPU.

direct mode instruction – instruction in which the operand is the data contained at the address specified in the address field of the instruction.

DMA – see direct memory access.

DMA controller – a device that performs bus arbitration.

DRAM – dynamic random access memory.

dynamic memory – memory that uses a capacitor to store logic 1s and 0s, and that must be refreshed periodically to restore the charge lost due to capacitive discharge.

effective instruction – the instruction created by the parameters to a one instruction, or a sequence of one instructions.

exception – error or other special condition that arise during program execution.

execute – process of sequencing through the steps in micromemory corresponding to a particular macroinstruction.

fetch – the process of retrieving a macroinstruction from main memory and placing it in the instruction register.

fetch-execute cycle – the process of continuously fetching and executing macroinstructions from main memory.

finite state automaton – a mathematical model consisting of a set of states, one of which is an initial state and others are terminal and non-terminal states, an alphabet and a transition function which maps a state and a letter from the alphabet into a new state. Also known as Moore finite state automaton (machine). A Mealy finite state automaton emits an output symbol from an alphabet of outputs with each transition.

flush – in pipelined architectures, the act of emptying the pipeline when branching occurs.

FSA – see finite state automaton.

FSM – see finite state automaton.

general register – CPU internal memory that is addressable in the address field of certain macroinstructions.

hypercube processors – a processor configuration that is similar to the linear array processor except that each processor element communicates data along a number of other higher dimensional pathways.

immediate mode instruction – an instruction in which the operand is an integer.

implied mode instruction – an instruction involving one or more specific memory locations or registers that are implicitly defined in the operation performed by instruction.

indirect mode instruction – instruction where the operand field is a memory location containing the address of the address of the operand.

instruction register – holds the opcode of the instruction that is currently being executed.

instruction parameterization – creating an effective instruction by selecting parameters to the one instruction.

instruction sequencing – using multiple one instructions sequentially to create a new instruction.

instruction synthesis – the process of creating an instruction from other instructions.

interrupt controller – a complex circuit that masks, latches, and prioritizes external interrupt signals.

interrupt – a hardware signal that initiates an event.

interrupt handler location – memory location containing the starting address of an interrupt-handler routine. The program counter is automatically loaded with its address when an interrupt occurs.

interrupt register – register containing a big map of all pending (latched) interrupts.

interrupt return location – memory location where the contents of the program counter is saved when the CPU processes an interrupt.

interrupt vector – register that contains the identity of the highest-priority interrupt request.

linear array processor – a processor organized so that multiple instructions of the same type can be executed in parallel.

machine code – binary instructions that affect specific computer operations. Also called machine language.

macrocode – see macroinstruction.

macroinstruction – binary program code stored in the main memory of the computer. Also called macrocode.

main memory – memory that is directly addressable by the CPU.

MAR – see memory address register.

mask register – a register that contains a bit map either enabling or disabling specific interrupts.

MDR – see memory data register.

memory address register (MAR) – holds the memory address to be read from or written to in the next memory bus cycle.

memory data register (MDR) – holds the data that was read from or is to be written to the memory address contained in the MAR in the next memory cycle.

mesh processor – a processor configuration that is similar to the linear array processor except that each processor element also communicates data north and south.

microcode – a sequence of binary instructions corresponding to a particular macroinstruction. Also called microinstructions.

microcontroller – a computer system that is programmable via microcode.

microinstructions – see microcode.

micromemory – a memory store that contains the microinstructions that form the complex logic of each macroinstruction.

microprogram – sequence of microcode stored in micromemory.

Multiplexer (mux) – a device used to route multiple lines onto fewer lines.

MUX – see multiplexer.

nonvolatile memory – memory whose contents are preserved upon removing power.

non-von Neumann architecture – an architecture that does not use the stored program, serial fetch-execute cycle model.

NOP – a macroinstruction that does not change the state of the computer.

object code – a specific collection of machine instructions.

opcode – the operation or instruction to be executed.

operand – a parameter of an instruction.

operandam – the first parameter of an instruction.

operandum – the second parameter of an instruction.

operative – the notion that an instruction in a processor manipulates the data.

PC – see program counter.

pipelining – a technique used to speed processor execution that relies on the fact that fetching the instruction is only one part of the fetch-execute cycle, and that it can overlap with different parts of the fetch-execute cycle for other instructions.

postfix notation – the result of building a binary parse tree with operands at the leaves and operations at the roots, and then traversing it in post-order fashion.

preempt – a condition that occurs when a higher-priority task interrupts a lower-priority task.

primary memory – see main memory.

processing elements – the individual processors in a multiprocessing system such as a systolic or wavefront architecture.

program counter (PC) – points to the next instruction in main memory to be executed.

propagation delay – the contribution to interrupt latency due to limitation in switching speeds of digital devices and in the transit time of electron across wires.

reduced instruction set computer (RISC) – architecture characterized by a small instruction set with limited addressing modes and a large number of general purpose registers.

register direct mode instruction – instruction in which the operand address is kept in a register named in the operand field of the instruction.

resultant – the third parameter for an instruction.

RISC – see reduced instruction set computer.

scratch pad memory – CPU internal memory used for intermediate results.

self-modifying code – code that can actually change itself; for example, by taking advantage of the fact that the opcodes of certain instructions may differ by only one bit.

speculative execution – in multiprocessing systems, a situation that involves an idle processor optimistically and predictively executing code in the next process block, as long as there is no dependency in that process block on code that could be running on other processors.

SRAM – static random-access memory.

stack – a first-in-ast-out data structure.

stack machine – computer architecture in which the instructions are centered on an internal memory store called a stack.

static memory – memory that does not rely on capacitive charge to store binary data.

stack pointer – points to top of an internal or external stack structure.

status register – contains control information that is generated by prior execution of instructions.

systolic processor – multiprocessing architecture that consists of a large number of uniform processors connected in an array topology.

transputer – a fully self-sufficient, multiple instruction set, von Neumann processor, designed to be connected to other transputers.

trap – internal interrupt caused by the execution of a certain instruction.

vector processor – see linear array processor.

von Neumann bottleneck – a situation in which the serial fetch and execution of instructions limits overall execution speed.

wavefront processor – a multiprocessing architecture that consists of an array of identical processors, each with its own local memory, and connected in a nearest-neighbor topology.

XOR closure – the set of operations using logical exclusive-or that is closed always with even 0's or 1's.

REFERENCES

"... and there came a great voice out of the temple of heaven, from the throne, saying, it is done."

Revelation 16:17, King James Version Holy Bible.

[Aho85] Aho, Alfred V., Sethi, Ravi, and Ullman, Jeffrey D. Compilers: Principles, Techniques, and Tools. Addison-Wesley, Reading, MA, 1985.

[Amdahl67] Amdahl, G.M. "Validity of the single-processor approach to achieving large scale computing capabilities." *Proceedings of the AFIPS*. Volume 30 (Atlantic City, N.J., Apr. 18-20). AFIPS Press, Reston, Va., 1967, pp. 483-485.

[Andrews90] Andrews, Gregory A. Foundations of Multithreaded, Parallel, and Distributed Programming. Addison-Wesley, Reading, MA, 1990.

[Armstrong00] Armstrong, James R. and F. Gail Gray. VHDL Design Representation and Synthesis 2nd Edition. Prentice-Hall, Upper Saddle River, NJ. 2000.

[Arnold96] Arnold, Marnix, and Lamberts, Reinoud, and Corporaal, Henk. "High Performance Image Processing Using TTAs," *Proceedings of Second Annual Conference of ASCI*, Lomnel, Belgium, June 1996.

[Backus78] Backus, John. "Can Programming Be Liberated from the von Neumann Style? A Functional Style and Its Algebra of Programs." *Communications of the ACM*, Volume 21, Number 8, August 1978, pp 613-641.

[Baker85] Baker, J. E. "Adaptive Selection Methods for Genetic Algorithms," *Proceedings of the International Conference Genetic Algorithms and Their Applications*, Pittsburgh, PA. 1985, pp. 101-111.

[Bell82] Bell, C. Gordon, Siewiorek, Daniel P., and Newell, Allen. Computer Structures: Readings and Examples. McGraw-Hill, New York, NY. 1982.

[Blaauw97] Blaauw, Gerrit A. and Brooks Jr., Frederick P. Computer Architecture: Concepts and Evolution. Addison-Wesley, Reading, MA. 1997.

[Blickle95] Blickle, Tobias and Thiele, Lothar. "A Comparison of Selection Schemes Used in Genetic Algorithms." *Technical Report 11, Computer Engineering and Communication Networks Lab (TIK)*, Swiss Federal Institute of Technology (ETH) Zurich, Gloriastrasse 35, CH-8092 Zurich, 1995.

[Böhm66] Böhm, Corrado and Jacopini, Giuseppe. "Flow Diagrams, Turing Machines and Languages with Only Two Formation Rules." *Communications of the ACM*, Volume 9, Number 5, May 1966.

[Carroll93] Carroll, Paul. The Big Blues: The Unmaking of IBM. Crown Publishers, New York, NY. 1993.

[Church36] Church, A. "An Unsolvable Problem of Elementary Number Theory," *American Mathematics*, Volume 58, 1936, pp. 345-263.

[Corporaal97] Corporaal, Henk. Microprocessor Architectures: From VLIW to TTA. John Wiley, New York. December 1997.

[Corporaal95] Corporaal, Henk, and Hoogerbrugge, Jan. "Code Generation for Transport Triggered Architectures" in Code Generation for Embedded Processor. Kluwer Academic Publishers, Boston, MA, 1995, pp. 240-259.

[Cringley92] Cringley, Robert X. Accidental Empires: How the Boys of Silicon Valley Build their Empires, Battle Foreign Competition, and Still Can't Get a Date. Addison-Wesley, Reading, MA. 1992.

[Dick98] Dick, Chris "Computing Multidimensional," *Proceedings of The 8th International Conference on Signal Processing Applications and Technology*, Toronto, Sept. 12-16, 1998.

[Dinman70] Dinman, Saul. "The Direct Function Processor Concept for System Control." *Computer Design Magazine*, March 1970.

[Dougherty88] Dougherty, E. R., and Giardina, C. R. Morphological Methods in Image and Signal Processing. Prentice Hall, Upper Saddle River, NJ, 1988.

[Draper02] Draper, Bruce A. et al, "Accelerated Image Processing on FPGAs," online technical publication http://www.cs.colostate.edu/cameron/Publications/draper_tip02.pdf, accessed May 2002.

[Feitelson02] Feitelson, Dror G., and Treinin, Millet. "The Blueprint for Life?" *IEEE Computer,* July 2002, pp. 34-39.

[Floyd90] Floyd, Thomas. Digital Fundamentals, 4th Edition. Merrill Publishing Company, Columbus, OH. 1990.

[Flynn96] Flynn, Michael J. and Rudd, Kevin W. "Parallel Architectures." *ACM Computing Surveys,* Volume 28, Number 1. March, 1996.

[Flynn72] Flynn, M., "Some Computer Organizations and Their Effectiveness." *IEEE Transactions on Computing,* Volume C-21, 1972, pp. 94.

[Flynn66] Flynn M. J., "Very High-Speed Computing Systems." *Proceedings of the IEEE,* Volume 54, Number 12, December 1966, pp. 1901-1909.

[Gilreath03] Gilreath, William F., and Laplante, Phillip A. "A One Instruction Computing Paradigm for Biological Computing." to appear, *International Journal of Computer Research,* 2003.

[Gustafson88] Gustafson, John. "Reevaluating, Amdahl's Law." *Communications of the ACM,* Volume 31, Number 5, May 1988, pp. 532-533.

[Hennessy98] Hennessy, John, and Patterson, David. Computer Organization and Design: The Hardware/Software Interface. 2nd Edition. Morgan-Kaufmann, San Francisco, CA. 1998.

[Hennessy96] Hennessy, John and Patterson, David. Computer Architecture: A Quantitative Approach. 2nd Edition. Morgan-Kaufmann, San Francisco, CA. 1996.

[Hennie77] Hennie, Fred. Introduction to Computability. Addison-Wesley, Reading, MA, 1977.

[Hillis98] Hillis, W. Daniel. The Pattern on the Stone. Basic Books, New York, New York, 1998.

[Hillis85] Hillis, W. Daniel. The Connection Machine. MIT Press, Cambridge, MA. 1985.

[Holland75] Holland, J. Adaptation in Natural and Artificial and Natural Systems, University of Michigan Press, Ann Arbor, MI, 1975.

[Hoare62] Hoare, C.A.R. "Quicksort." *The Computer Journal,* Number 5. 1962, pp. 10-15.

[Hutter02] Hutter, Marcus. "Fitness Uniform Selection to Preserve Genetic Diversity." *Proceedings of the 2002 Congress on Evolutionary Computation* (CEC-2002), pp. 783-788

[Inoue97] Inoue, T., Sano, M. and Takahashi, Y. "Design of a Processing Element of a SIMD Computer for Genetic Algorithms," *High Performance and Computing on the Information Superhighway*, HPC, 1997, pp. 688-691.

[Jones88a] Jones, Douglas. "The Ultimate RISC." *ACM Computer Architecture News*. Volume 16, Number 3, June 1988. pp. 48-55.

[Jones88b] Jones, Douglas. "A Minimal CISC." *ACM Computer Architecture News*. Volume 16, Number 3, June 1988. pp. 56-63.

[Laplante03] Laplante, Phillip A., and Gilreath, Will. "One Instruction Set Computers for Image Processing," to appear *Journal of VLSI Signal Processing Systems*, 2003.

[Laplante02] Laplante, Phillip A., and Gilreath, William. "Single Instruction Set Architectures for Image Processing," *Proceedings of Reconfigurable Technology*, part of *ITCOM*, SPIE, July 2002, pp 20-29.

[Laplante01] Laplante, Phillip A. (Editor). Dictionary of Computer Science Engineering and Technology, CRC Press, Boca Raton, FL, 2001.

[Laplante91a] Laplante, P.A. "A Single Instruction Computer Architecture and Its Application in Image Processing," *Proceedings of Intelligent Robots and Computer Vision X: Biological, Neural Net, and 3-D Methods*, Volume 1608, Boston, MA, November 1991, pp. 226-235.

[Laplante91b] Laplante, Phillip. "An Improved Conditional Branching Scheme for a Single Computer Instruction Architecture." *SIGForth Newsletter*. Volume 3, Number 1. Summer 1991.

[Laplante90] Laplante, P.A. "A Novel Single Instruction Computer Architecture," *ACM Computer Architecture News*, Volume 18, Number 4, December 1990, pp. 22-23.

[McCurry02] McCurry, Peter, Morgan, Fearghal, and Kilmartin, Liam. "Xilinx FPGA Implementation of a Pixel Processor for Object Detection Applications." *Xilinx Technical papers*, www.celoxica.com/products/technical_papers/academic_papers/paperPMcC.PDF, accessed May 2002.

[Maclennan99] Maclennan, Bruce J. Principles of Programming Languages. 3rd Edition. Oxford University Press, New York, NY. 1999.

[Malone95] Malone, Michael S. The Microprocessor a Biography. Springer-Verlag, New York, NY, 1995.

[Margulis90] Margulis, Neal. i860 Microprocessor Architecture. Osborne McGraw-Hill, Berkeley, California, 1990.

[Martel89] Martel, Charles U. and Gusfield, Dan. "A Fast Parallel Quicksort Algorithm." *Information Processing Letters*, Volume 30, Number 2, January 1989, pp. 97-102.

[Martin01] Martin, Peter. "A Hardware Implementation of a Genetic Programming System Using FPGAs and Handel-C." *Genetic Programming and Evolvable Machines*, Volume 2, 2001, pp. 317-343.

[Mavaddat88] Mavaddat, F. and Parhami, P. "URISC: The Ultimate Reduced Instruction Set Computer." *International Journal of Electrical Engineering Education.* Volume 25, Number 4, October 1988, pp. 327-334.

[Moore91] Moore, S. W., and Morgan, G. "The Recursive MOVE Machine: r-move." *IEE Colloquium on RISC Architectures and Applications*, 1991, pp. 3/1 – 3/5.

[Moore65] Moore, Gordon. "Cramming more Components onto Integrated Circuits." *Electronics*, Volume 38, Number 8, April 1965.

[Pennicott02] Pennicott, Katie. "'DNA' Computer Cracks Code." *Physics Web*, http://physicsweb.org/article/news/6/3/11, accessed 3/18/2002.

[Prasad89] Prasad, N. S. IBM Mainframes Architecture and Design. Intertext Publications, New York, NY, 1989.

[Radin99] Radin, George. "801 and the PowerPC." *IEEE Computer.* Volume 32, Number 11. November 1999.

[Radin83] Radin, George. "The 801 Minicomputer." *IBM Journal Research and Development*, May 1983. pp. 237-246.

[Reif02] Reif, J. "The Emergence of the Discipline of Biomolecular Computing in the US." *New Generation Computing*, Volume 20, 2002, pp. 1-23.

[Rojas98] Rojas, Raúl. "How to Make Zuse's Z3 A Universal Computer." *IEEE Annals of Computing.* Volume 20, Number 3, July/September 1998, pp. 51-54.

[Rojas96] Rojas, Raúl. "Conditional Branching is not Necessary for Universal Computation in von Neumann Computer." *Journal of Universal Computer Science.* Volume 2, Number 11. 1996. pp. 756-767.

[Roth92] Roth, Charles H. Jr. Fundamentals of Logic Design. 4th Edition. West Publishing, New York, NY. 1992.

[Scanlon80] Scanlon, Leo J. 6502 Software Design. Howard W. Sams & Company. Indianapolis, IN. 1980.

[Sebesta96] Sebesta, Robert. Concepts of Programming Languages, 3rd Edition. Addison-Wesley, Reading, MA. 1996.

[Shurkin96] Shurkin, Joel. Engines of the Mind: The Evolution of the Computer from Mainframes to Microprocessors. W.W. Norton, New York, NY. 1996.

[Tabak80] Tabak, Daniel and G. Jack Lipovski. "MOVE Architecture in Digital Controllers." *IEEE Transactions on Computers*, Volume 29, Number 2, 1980, pp. 180-190.

[Tabak96] Tabak, Daniel. RISC Systems and Applications. Research Studies Press, LTD, Somerset, England. 1996.

[Todman02] Todman, Tim, and Luk, Wayne. "Reconfigurable Designs for Ray Tracing," *Xilinx Technical papers*, http://www.celoxica.com/products/technical_papers/academic_papers/Reconfigurable%20Designs%20for%20Ray%20Tracing.pdf, accessed May 2002.

[Turing36] Turing, Alan M. "On Computable Numbers, with an Application to the Entscheidungsproblem." *Proceedings of London Mathematical Society*. Volume 2, Number 42, pp. 230-265. 1936.

[Turley02] Turley, Jim. "Design Your Own Microprocessor." *Circuit Cellar*, www.circuitcellar.com/library/print/0502/2.asp, Issue 142, May 2002.

[Twardowski94], Twardowski, Kirk. "An Associative Architecture for Genetic Algorithm-Based Machine Learning." *Computer*, Volume 27, Issue 11, November 1994, pp. 27-38.

[van der Poel59] van der Poel, W.L. "ZEBRA, A Simple Binary Computer." *Proceedings ICIP* (UNESCO, Paris), 1959, pp. 361-65.

[van der Poel56a] van der Poel, W. L. "The Essential Types of Operations in an Automatic Computer." *Nachrichtentechnische Fachberichte*, Volume 4, 1956, pp. 144-145.

[van der Poel56b] van der Poel, W.L. The Logical Principles of Some Simple Computers. PhD Thesis. University of Amsterdam, 1956. Reprinted, The Hague, The Netherlands: Excelsior, 1962.

[van der Poel52] van der Poel. W. L. "A Simple Electronic Digital Computer." *Applied Science Research*, Section B, Volume 2, 1952, pp. 367-400.

[von Neumann45] von Neumann, John. "First Draft Report on the EDVAC." Contract W-670-ORD-4926, Moore School of Electrical Engineering, University of Pennsylvania, 1945. *Reprinted in IEEE Annals of the History of Computing*, Volume 15, Number 4, 1993, pp. 27-75.

[Wilkes53] Wilkes, Maurice V. and Stringer, J.B. "Microprogramming and the Design of the Control Circuits in an Electronic Digital Computer." *Proceedings Cambridge Philosophical Society*, Volume 49, Number 2, 1953, pp. 230-238.

[Wilkes51] Wilkes, Maurice V. "The Best Way to Design an Automatic Calculating Machine" *Presented at Manchester University Computer Inaugural Conference*, July 1951. Reprinted in Daniel P. Siewiorek, Bell, and Newell 1982, pp. 158-163.

[Xilinx98] Xilinx, Inc. Core Solutions Databook, San Jose, CA, 1998.

[Xilinx97] Xilinx, Inc. Synopsys (XSI) Synthesis and Simulation Design Guide, San Jose, CA, 1997.

[Xu89] Xu, Jianning. "The Optimal Implementation of Morphological Operations On Neighborhood Connected Array Processors." *IEEE Computer Society Conference on Computer Vision and Pattern Recognition*, 1989, pp. 166–171.

Index

About the Authors

William Gilreath is an independent software engineer, researcher, and developer. He has several years of software experience with C/C++ and Java on the Unix and Windows platforms.

Mr. Gilreath has written articles and book reviews for *IEEE Concurrency* and *IEEE Distributed Systems* online. His technical interests include the Web, software development, distributed systems, minimalist computer architectures, and programming languages.

He holds B.S. degree in Computer Science from Mississippi State University, where he has also done graduate work. He also privately consults as a software engineer and developer.

Dr. Phillip A. Laplante is Associate Professor of Software Engineering at The Pennsylvania State University's Great Valley School of Graduate Professional Studies in Malvern, Pennsylvania. Before joining the university, he was a professor and senior academic administrator at several other colleges and universities.

In addition to his academic career, Dr. Laplante spent almost eight years as a software engineer and project manager working on avionics (including the Space Shuttle), CAD, and software test systems. He has authored or edited 14 books and more than 100 other papers, articles, and editorials. He co-founded the journal *Real-Time Imaging* (Academic Press), which he edited for five years, and he created and edits two book series.

Dr. Laplante received his B.S., M.Eng., and Ph.D. in Computer Science, Electrical Engineering, and Computer Science, respectively, from Stevens Institute of Technology and an MBA from the University of Colorado. He is a senior member of IEEE and a member of numerous professional societies, program committees, and boards. He is a licensed professional engineer in Pennsylvania.